D1008330

PROPERTY OF
NATIONAL UNIVERSITY
LIBRARY

HELPING OTHERS
HELP THEMSELVES
A Guide to Counseling Skills

JOHN W. LOUGHARY

THERESA M. RIPLEY

Professors of Counseling
University of Oregon

McGraw-Hill Book Company

New York   St. Louis   San Francisco   Auckland   Bogotá   Düsseldorf
Johannesburg   London   Madrid   Mexico   Montreal   New Delhi   Panama
Paris   São Paulo   Singapore   Sydney   Tokyo   Toronto

HELPING OTHERS HELP THEMSELVES
A Guide to Counseling Skills

Copyright © 1979 by McGraw-Hill, Inc. All rights reserved. Printed in the United States of America. No part of this publication may be reproduced, stored in a retrieval system, or transmitted, in any form or by any means, electronic, mechanical, photocopying, recording, or otherwise, without the prior written permission of the publisher.

3 4 5 6 7 8 9 0   DODO   8 3 2 1

This books was set in Times Roman by The Total Book (ECU/BTI).
The editors were Robert G. Manley and Helen Kelly; the production supervisor was Dominick Petrellese.
R. R. Donnelley & Sons Company was printer and binder.

Library of Congress Cataloging in Publication Data

Loughary, John William, date
   Helping others help themselves.

   Bibliography: p.
   Includes index.
   1. Counseling. 2. Helping behavior. I. Ripley,
Theresa M., joint author. II. Title.
BF637.C6L67   158   78-26946
ISBN 0-07-038756-7

Contents

Preface

How often have you said or heard the remark, "I'd like to help, but I don't know what to do." Helping is an important aspect of relationships. It is a means of showing concern, interest, affection, and other positive feelings. The desire to be helpful is part of our culture.

But, people's ability to be helpful often falls short of their desires. Why? Shouldn't helping come naturally? For some people it certainly seems to happen naturally. They know the appropriately helpful thing to do or say at just the right moment. It is also possible to learn to be helpful.

Our contention is that one useful way to think about helping is in terms of outcomes and tools. The intended results of helping are various outcomes or changes for the person receiving help. To assist in bringing about these outcomes, the helper can use relatively specific procedures and ideas. In short, if you want to be maximally helpful, understand your purpose and have the appropriate skills for pursuing it.

Our purpose in writing *Helping Others Help Themselves* is to describe the skills and ideas in a demystified manner and with sufficient clarity so that they can be used effectively as helping tools. With a wide variety of helpers in mind, we have selected illustrations from many kinds of relationships and situations.

The helping tools described in the following pages are not unique to us. They have been used in one form or another by counselors, parents, teachers, supervisors, psychologists and others. The first version of the materials in the book was published in mimeographed form in 1973 and was used in a variety of courses and workshops. User suggestions led to a revised version published in 1975 by United Learning Corporation. Following more user evaluations, further revisions were made and new material added to produce the present book.

We want to emphasize that *Helping Others Help Themselves* is about assisting people to reach goals, gain satisfaction, and resolve issues which are part of the real world for most of us. It is not about doing psychotherapy or professional counseling. Complex psychological problems require professional assistance. Chapter 7 describes a variety of sources of such help.

Course and workshop participants from a variety of helping professions made suggestions for this book. We appreciate their assistance. We are also grateful to Ruth Brewer and June Wyant, both special collections librarians, who provided some of the annotated references in Chapter 10. Helen Kelly was McGraw-Hill's development editor. She questioned, suggested, nudged, and challenged our helping concept—a subject to which she has a strong commitment. She was very helpful. Special thanks to Sally George for her skill, patience, and involvement in helping produce the actual manuscript. With the help of these good people acknowledged, we must note that total responsibility for the content of the book is ours.

John W. Loughary
Theresa M. Ripley

One | An Overview of Helping

ALL OF US ARE HELPERS

It's a pretty good bet that most every day of your life you assist other people in various ways. You may do simple things, such as helping someone find postal rates or assisting a shut-in to find transportation. You may give instructions, loan a book, or encourage someone to write a letter to obtain information. To help others feel better, you may listen to a child complain about a teacher, a spouse describe a trying day, or an employee reveal marital problems. You may act as a sounding board for someone who is trying to decide where to take a vacation, or be a reflector for a friend who is confused and upset regarding a relationship, or serve as a target for someone who wants to express anger. You may teach Jim how to communicate concern more effectively, provide moral support for Joan doing her first job interview, or be a companion to Betty who was recently widowed. You may show a child how to camp, a retired person how to find recreation opportunities, or a young couple how to shop for a loan.

Helping is providing purposeful assistance to other people which makes their lives more pleasant, easier, less frustrating, or in some other way, more satisfying. Most every relationship you have involves the opportunity for helping. Think about your own relationships from the perspective of helping. Make a list of all the roles you play. Are you a friend? Employer? Supervisor? Parent? Spouse? Lover? Student? Uncle? Aunt? Brother? Sister? Grandparent? Son? Daughter? Companion? Information provider? Concerned citizen? Committee member? Neighbor? Club member? Teammate? Roommate? What else?

Visualize each relationship and ask the question, "Does this relationship involve assisting others?" To what extent do you try to inform people, make them feel better, listen to their problems, suggest, make arrangements, teach, explain, criticize, and in other ways assist them?

In response to this self-inventory, you may find that you provide help within several relationships. Few people lead such isolated lives that they do not have daily opportunities to help. Thus, the question is not "Do we help?" but rather "How effective is our help?"

Some people seem to be much more effective helpers than others. And you may be more helpful in some kinds of situations than in others. You may, for example, be a good listener and thus helpful to people who want to express their feelings, but not very good at teaching people how to obtain information. You may be viewed as helpful by the neighbor's son and ignored as a resource by your own child. We can recognize that being helpful is not an all or nothing proposition, and that most of us can improve our helping skills.

ACQUIRING HELPING SKILLS

How do we acquire whatever helping skills we possess? Very few people receive training in helping. It's not a subject schools usually include in their curricula. For the most part, we acquire helping skills by learning from our experiences. We learn many other skills in the same way. Walking, talking, playing, as well as negotiating, being persuasive, and providing leadership, all require skills which we learn, in part, from our experiences. The same can be said about helping, and it is obvious that you have acquired many helping skills this way.

You can also acquire helping skills in a more formal or structured manner. People who want to be professional helpers, such as counselors, social workers, and ministers, take advanced course work in helping skills.

People preparing for other occupations in which providing assistance with personal concerns is not the primary emphasis, but still an important consideration, also learn helping skills by taking courses. People in law enforcement, dental and medical occupations, and sales, are examples. Some colleges offer courses in specific kinds of helping skills for nonprofessionals. Examples include courses in parent education, moral education, caring for elderly people, assisting people with various handicaps, and developing communication skills.

Taking courses with qualified instructors is undoubtedly the most effective way to acquire helping skills. Instructors can provide supervision and can also individualize learning to each person's particular needs and interests.

Even though the ideal method of acquiring helping skills is by taking courses, you can also teach yourself. In order to take the self-taught approach, you need to meet two requirements. First, you need descriptions and illustrations of the helping skills you want to learn. Second, you must practice the skills. This book speaks to both requirements. *Helping Others Help Themselves* contains descriptions and illustrations of helping tools and suggestions for practicing their use.

The purpose of this book is to assist you to become a more effective helper. In order to do that, you will have opportunities to examine and practice a variety of helping skills. Our contention is pretty straightforward. If you will do the things suggested in this book, you can probably become a more effective helper. There is also a possibility that you may not. You may be a pretty effective helper already, and find what we have to say basic. Or, you may be someone whose values, interests, and personality are not geared to helping others. We think that most people can improve their helping skills, but that is not to say that they *ought* to do so.

Some people confuse helping others with satisfying their own desires. You are probably not such a person. For those who may be, there is little we can do except to urge finding other solutions to your problems. Certainly people do gain much personal satisfaction from helping, but hopefully within a context which values and respects those receiving help. Helping for the wrong reasons means using the problems and misery of other people for selfish purposes. This ranges from idle curiosity to complex manipulations cloaked as helping efforts. We will look more closely at the issue of reasons for helping and not helping in Chapter 3.

In the remainder of this chapter we describe and illustrate the helping process. The helping process is a series of events which assists people to make desired changes. They may change, for example, from feeling angry to feeling calm, from being confused about an issue to understanding it, or from being uncertain to certain. The helping process has a beginning and an end. It involves a person with a concern, and a helper who uses information, concepts, and skills.

If that seems complex, don't be put off. Much helping is done without thinking about it. It's second nature. You automatically offer a ride to someone, or phone when you know a friend may be under stress. Relatively routine helpful acts such as these make life easier, and to examine them in detail would be pointless.

Sometimes, however, an action intended to be helpful is not. It can even have the opposite effect and make matters worse. Why? Because a fairly complicated situation may be involved, and the would-be helper doesn't know how to identify the various things which might be done, nor how to purposefully decide what to do. Helping, in other words, frequently requires more than good intentions.

THE HELPING PROCESS

Prior to helping, it is important to understand the situation. One way for you to understand is to learn to view a helping situation in terms of the helping process. The process is illustrated in Figure 1. It has three main aspects:

Problem

Assisting

Outcomes

The process begins when someone has a *problem* or concern; that is, a person believes that "Things are not as I want them to be." The "things" may be feelings, other people, financial conditions, or any of a multitude of factors.

Assisting involves one person using helping tools and helping strategies directed at another person's concerns. Helping tools include *information* (e.g., name of credit union), *ideas* (e.g., suggesting a new way to resolve a

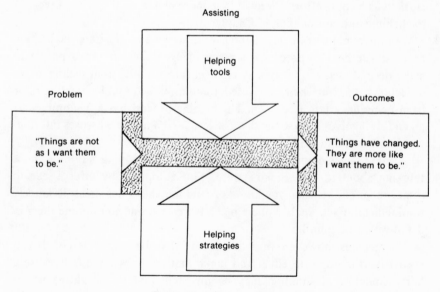

Figure 1 Helping process

parent-child conflict), and *skills* (e.g., clarifying a complex idea). A *strategy* is a plan for using the tools.

The helping process ends when a desired *outcome* has occurred and the person being helped can say, "Things have changed—they are more like I want them to be."

Let's take a look at the way these three aspects of the helping process operate when you decide to be a helper. The range of *problems* or "Things are not as I want them to be" situations is nearly endless. There are, of course, various ways of classifying problems. We can use labels to categorize various kinds of "Things are not as I want them to be" situations. These labels include loneliness, depression, confusion, frustration, anger, poverty, failure, conflict, ignorance, sadness, helplessness, disorientation, boredom, fatigue, confusion, anxiety, and skill deficiency. The conditions represented by these labels also vary tremendously in degree. Depression, for example, ranges from being "down in the dumps" to needing hospitalization. One person's loneliness may be overcome by a brief phone conversation while helping with another's may involve dealing with complex feelings of rejection and alienation. Ignorance may be erased by a few facts or can require months of learning.

Because of the great range of problems and the possible complexity, problem labels are not very useful as we write about helping. Consequently, we will avoid using labels as much as possible. Instead, we will focus on the feelings, thoughts, and behavior which are involved in helping situations.

When we speak of the problem aspect of the helping process, therefore, we try to be as specific as possible. So, instead of saying, "John is depressed," we would indicate that "John would like to change negative feelings about his performance in school." Instead of stating that Molly is lonely, we would say, "Molly would like to have people with whom she could share activities."

Describing conditions has two advantages over labeling them. First, it clarifies the changes needed to bring about the desired outcomes. Second, it provides you with a better basis for deciding whether or not you have the appropriate skills to be helpful.

Assisting, from the helper's point of view, involves helping tools (concepts, skills, and information) and helping strategies (a plan for using the tools to help obtain the desired outcomes). Most of the book is concerned with the assisting aspect of the process.

Outcomes of helping may be clearly defined at one extreme, or vague at the other, but in all cases outcomes are desired changes in the life of the person being helped. An outcome, for example, might simply be a change from feeling discouraged to not discouraged; or a change from a state of indecision to a state of having made a decision. Examples of more tangible outcomes are obtaining training or a job, getting off drugs or alcohol, having more plesant relationships with one's child, improving one's job performance, or making more satisfactory use of leisure time. We will discuss outcomes in Chapter 2.

We can illustrate the three aspects of the helping process—problem, assistance, outcomes—with a situation in which the outcome for the person being helped was increased understanding. The change is a result of the helper doing active listening. You have probably experienced it. Recall a situation in which another person listened to you describe your concerns or troubles and as a result you said to yourself something such as, "Gee I feel better" or "Thank God, somebody understands me." Now recall a situation to which your reaction was, "Why did I tell them all of that? I feel worse—wish I could have shut up!"

Chances are that the first situation involved active listening. The person who was helpful used what we refer to as active listening tools with the intention of helping you express your concerns, and the second listener did not.

The following example of helping by using active listening involves two friends, Jim and Bill:

"I feel guilty as hell," Jim confessed. "Last night my nineteen-year-old son and I got into an argument about his using the car—I shoved him. Didn't really solve anything—just put us farther apart. How can you talk to kids without losing your temper?"

"It's sometimes difficult, isn't it?" Bill reflected.

"It sure is but I still lose my temper. I guess I'll try to talk with him again tonight—but I know there'll be a hassle—it's the same every time."

"You usually try to have these discussions in the evening?" Bill asked.

"Yeah. It's not an ideal time. I'm tired and he usually wants to get out some place. And there are always other members of the family around. But when else? Before work in the morning is just as bad."

"No time at home seems very appropriate," Bill noted.

"Not so far, but maybe that's part of the problem. I mean maybe we need to get on neutral ground in order to talk," Jim speculated.

"That would take some effort, probably."

"Some—but not that much," replied Jim. I suppose I could take the kid to lunch, or on a drive. You know, I think I'll try that."

"You'll suggest that to your son?" Bill asked carefully.

"You're right—it would be better to get his agreement, wouldn't it?" Jim said, responding to his friend's implied suggestion.

"Well, at least the two of you would begin by agreeing that there is a problem which needs to be resolved," commented Bill.

In this example, Bill used a couple of active listening tools. First, he conveyed acceptance of his friend's concern by acknowledging the difficulty of the situation—but without taking sides. *Conveying acceptance* is a basic listening tool. It conveys to the speaker that both he and what he has to say are important and worthy of another person's attention. Indicating acceptance also acknowledges your willingness to listen and encourages the speaker to continue.

Clarification is another active listening tool. Bill asked a question regarding the time of the discussions which helped Jim clarify part of the situation. In answering the question, Jim realized that the time and place of his attempted conversations with his son were not the best. Bill used the tools of acceptance and clarification in the process of helping, and Jim thought of a new plan for talking with his son. Bill could have responded to Jim in ways which would not have been helpful. For instance, he could have taken sides regarding Jim's shoving his son, or he could have encouraged a general gripe session about how today's teenagers are confused and alienated. In our judgment, neither response would likely have been helpful because they would have been nonpurposeful responses to Jim's statement. Active listening, while probably appearing to be casual, is thoughtful, deliberate helping. Even though active listening doesn't require an intense stare, a couch and a Viennese accent, it is, nevertheless, purposeful helping.

In this illustration of the helping process involving Jim and Bill, one person had concerns (things were not as Jim wanted them to be), another person used helping tools in a considered, purposeful manner and outcomes resulted (things are more like Jim wanted them to be). Essentially, that's the helping process. It is obviously often more complicated than the example, as much of this book illustrates.

A great deal has been made in both popular books and the professional counseling literature about the importance of the "helping relationship." It is argued by some that the most important aspect of offering help to another person is the quality of the human relationship between the two people. There is no doubt that the quality of the relationship is important. If I see you as overbearing, conceited, and pompous, you probably won't be very helpful to me. If, in contrast, I see you as a warm, accepting, understanding person who is concerned, then help may be on the way. Through our relationship, you may give me the strength to face my problems. And that is good. But, if, having established the favorable relationship you should also help me change in a more substantive manner, I would be much more appreciative and your time much better spent.

A warm, accepting, nonevaluative relationship is usually an important condition of helping, but it is seldom sufficient. For those of us who, for whatever reasons, are often in positions to provide help, the most humanitarian thing we can do is to assure ourselves that we have helping skills.

There is one additional concern to be treated to complete our overview of the helping process and that is problem ownership. When we suggest that helping often offers the possibility of doing something for other people, this does not imply that you take over any of their responsibilities. Each of us has the responsibility for our own actions. That is an important point. One moves into a helping relationship with the clear intention of moving out as soon as appropriate. As we will illustrate later, it is sometimes important to clarify the issue of "problem ownership" with the person you are helping. You may want to make it clear that you are not inviting a partnership arrangement.

As a helper you are a resource. People being helped may need to be reminded that the problems are theirs. The idea that no one else can solve our problems for us, as well as the increased freedom associated with directing one's own life, are important concepts. If you begin to assume part ownership of another person's problems, you can become preoccupied with it. You may worry about a problem which really isn't yours. If worrying about your own problems is nonproductive, then worrying about someone else's is foolish, and who wants to be helped by a fool?

Two | Outcomes and Tools

OUTCOMES

This chapter describes the outcomes of helping and provides an overview of helping tools. We begin with outcomes, because when it's all said and done, results make the difference. Helping tools and procedures are important, as are your concern for others and your desire to be helpful. But without a clear understanding of the contribution you are trying to make, you have little basis for providing purposeful specific help. Being relatively specific about desired outcomes of helping enables you to be selective and more precise regarding your helping behavior. The helping tools and strategies which we will discuss and illustrate will allow the person being helped to achieve four kinds of outcomes. These are:

Changes in feeling states

Increased understanding

Decisions

Implementing decisions

These outcomes are not mutually exclusive; that is, one can be part of another. Let's examine each outcome briefly.

Change in Feeling States

Examples of feeling states are joy and anger. A feeling state is an emotional condition you experience for a period of time. It is more than a brief emotional reaction, and stronger or more specific than a mood. It may last for a part of an hour, a day, or several days or even longer. It is usually associated with a given event or experience. Sometimes the cause of a feeling state is clear to us, sometimes it is not. A feeling state may interfere seriously with our daily activities, or it may be pushed to the edge of awareness until the end of the day when we are no longer preoccupied with daily concerns and responsibilities. Negative feeling states are bothersome. Even though positive feeling states, such as joy and excitement, can cause temporary confusion, people seldom want to change them. The point we emphasize is that negative feeling states are psychologically uncomfortable, sometimes painful. Examples of negative feeling states include frustration, depression, anger, self-pity, resentment, jealousy, envy, loneliness, neglect, and rejection.

Any particular feeling state can be described in terms of its degree of positiveness or negativeness. Feeling states can also be described in regard to their intensity. In general, it is the placement of feeling states on the positive-negative and intensity continuums which determines their debilitating effect. Feelings which are neither very positive nor very negative, and feelings which are not intense, tend not to be debilitating. Change in feelings can be in degree as well as kind. Helping a person overcome debilitating loneliness may not require eliminating the feeling, which may be an unrealistic goal. Helping reduce the intensity of loneliness may eliminate its debilitating effect.

You may recognize the following pattern in which negative feeling states precipitate unproductive and unpleasant behavior. In the process of getting the family up and going one morning, John gets into an argument with his son, Mike. Both make several hostile statements to each other, and leave home with feelings of anger and frustration over the unresolved conflict. Mike is preoccupied with his anger and frustrated because he did not make his point more effectively to his father. During the day he cannot concentrate on a first-period math test and scores lower than he might have. Both his buddy and the first-period teacher observed that he seemed upset but neither asked about, nor did anything to help change, his feelings.

John, the father, is also angry and feels inadequate because he allowed the situation to degenerate into an ugly conflict. Preoccupied with his own feelings, he is inattentive during an early morning meeting, thus in part wasting his own time as well as that of his associates. Two coworkers noted before the meeting that John was upset, predicted that his feelings might have an impact on the meeting, but did nothing to help him change them or even acknowledge that the feelings existed.

While there was little that John or Mike could do about resolving their actual conflict during the day, they could have coped more effectively with their feelings about the conflict. Further, their friends and associates could have been helpful in changing their feelings. For example, Mike's teacher could have asked Mike if he were upset, thus giving him a chance to acknowledge his frustration. Similarly, John's coworkers could have given him an opportunity to acknowledge that he was upset. And note that in both cases it was their feelings, not the actual conflict, which was working to their disadvantage.

The distinction between events and reactions to events is not easy to make. What causes feeling states? Who or what brings them about? Other people or external events? Neither, actually. When we have negative feeling states, usually someone has violated our values or ignored our underlying assumptions. Our reaction is to feel. For example, imagine you have purchased a new coat and are very pleased with it. You hang it by your desk. The next thing you know a coworker has borrowed it and brings it back wet and wrinkled. Your reaction is anger. Did the coworker make you mad? No. You made yourself mad because a person ignored your assumption that no one should borrow your belongings without first obtaining your permission. Had you been a member of a communal group in which the idea of private property didn't exist, you wouldn't have reacted with anger to your coworker's behavior.

We cause our own feelings. If you are a nonsmoker and someone inconsiderately smokes in your living room and you become irritated, it is not they who have caused you irritation. Rather, you have made yourself irritated about what they did. Comics don't *make* you laugh. You cause yourself to be amused about what they said. Understanding that a negative feeling is one's own reaction to someone else's violation of one's values helps focus on the source over which one has the most control—oneself. Becoming upset over someone else's behavior usually isn't very useful or productive. Often there is little we can do to change another's behavior. It is usually more productive to focus on our own behavior than on that of others. In the coat episode, for example, explaining your values about private property to coworkers would be time-consuming and might create more problems in the process. A more effective solution would be to focus on your own behavior; hang your coat where it is not easily accessible to others.

Changing negative feeling states often involves helping people clarify underlying values and assumptions. There are tools which can assist people to clarify values and assumptions. As a result of clarification, they can turn from a preoccupation with negative feelings to action aimed at dealing with the circumstances to which they object. There are a variety of ways by which one person can help another change negative feeling states into neutral or even positive feeling states. Often the change in feelings can be accomplished without doing anything at all about the precipitating events or circumstances.

Increased Understanding

A second outcome of helping is increased understanding. Lack of understanding tends to be about three subjects: self, others, and circumstances. People do all kinds of foolish things which get them into painfully embarrassing situations because they don't understand themselves very well. Students who take courses which are too difficult, people who engage in business ventures which are excessively demanding, and marriage partners who make unrealistic promises are just a few causes of unhappiness which can be created by inadequate knowledge about oneself. There is no guarantee, obviously, that once we understand ourselves, we will act intelligently. Goodness knows there is certainly evidence to the contrary, but at least it's a start. Nor is self-understanding meant to deter one permanently from some course. One nice thing about humans is that they can learn and change once they understand.

Self-understanding is an ongoing challenge. We are constantly changing throughout the life span. It is easy for people to forget that their interests and values change. Marriage partners of ten years, for example, who try to resolve difficulties based on their initial values, may be doomed to disappointment. They probably have altered their values significantly during the ten years. Rather than trying to rebuild the old relationship, it would be more realistic to understand their current values and build a new relationship.

Much unhappiness can result from our failure to understand significant others in our life. Consider the number of disastrous family vacations due to father's being oblivious that no one else really wanted to go camping; the ineffective company reorganizations in which territorial rights were not understood; the damaged friendships resulting from invalid assumptions. Understanding significant others involves knowing their interests and values and their perceptions of us. Understanding others' feelings can be an especially difficult task because people tend not to be frank about how they feel about each other. Sometimes, when they are, they confuse being open with being obnoxious. Helpers, from more neutral third party stances and with the benefit of alternative perceptions, can use a number of tools to assist an individual to increase understanding of significant others.

The third kind of increased understanding is of environmental circumstances. Examples are laws, policies, and "how-to" information. Assisting a would-be high school dropout understand that there are five ways to earn a high school diploma, besides graduating from a regular high school, is an example of increasing understanding of circumstances.

Lack of understanding can be caused by incomplete information, inaccurate information, and misperception. In instances of incomplete and inaccurate information, assistance in seeking information can be very helpful. It is not unusual for people to be unaware that information relevant to their concerns exists. For example, free information regarding topics such as leisure activities, tax savings, product ratings, and family planning is readily available in most communities.

Increased understanding does not always require that the helper provide new information. It is sometimes a matter of assisting an individual to reorganize his perception of what is already known. The new perception can be a change in emphasis or the consideration of alternative explanations of a situation. Dave is a seventeen-year-old high school senior whose participation in "kegger parties" brings his parents into unpleasant confrontation with school officials. Dave's reaction to his parents' complaints and attempts to impose rules is increased anger and resentment. If, however, someone can help him understand that their concern is not that they consider his behavior as especially bad or undesirable in itself, but mostly resent the inconvenience it brings them, he will have a better basis for making decisions. Assuming that he values his parents' well-being, Dave's increased understanding of their concern may lead to his changing the situation, regardless of whether or not he feels any differently about their attempts to control him.

As just noted, a helper in this example would probably supply little, if any, new information to Dave. Instead the helper would rely on an ability to perceive the situation differently from the way Dave was viewing it. Lack of understanding often results when we get locked into a particular view of a situation, or from a preoccupation with some particular concern such as self-defense.

Helping people increase understanding of self, others, and circumstances, can be very beneficial. Information is power, and ignorance can be very restricting. In your own experiences, have you heard people explain why they made a mess of something by saying, "Gee, I didn't understand"?

Decisions

Another major outcome of helping is the making of decisions, and even more important, increased decision-making ability. A major source of unhappiness for many people is their inability to make decisions. Taken to an extreme, the inability to make decisions can render people almost totally unable to manage their lives effectively. Of course, all of us find some decisions difficult to make. That is normal, because important decisions by definition involve uncertainty. Many decisions involve complicated choices that have both positive and negative consequences. Thus some of the difficulty in making decisions is inherent in the decisions themselves and impossible to avoid. Part of the difficulty of making decisions, however, is often lack of decision-making skills—such things as identifying positive and negative outcomes of a decision, estimating the risks involved in alternative courses of action, realistically assessing our ability to "carry it off," and seeking out important information. Those skills can be learned.

Another problem associated with making decisions is being aware of when they can be made, and when they have been made unknowingly. We make so many decisions automatically that it is easy to overlook the importance of decision making in our lives. Ask most people to list important decisions and they refer to schooling, marriage, job choice, and major purchases such as a house, car, and appliances. While these are important, there are large numbers of additional decisions and nondecisions made each day. Think back to this morning, and review the first sixty minutes following your acting on the decision to get out of bed. Everything you did involved a decision or at least an opportunity to decide not to do it. That is, you didn't have to do any of the things you did (with a possible exception or two) during those sixty minutes. For the most part, we can be thankful that so many personal decisions are automatic. If we had to decide consciously about everything we do, life would be tiring, to say the least.

However, we can become so used to believing that decisions are automatic, that we lower our sensitivity to potentially important decision points in life. For example, suppose tomorrow you receive a letter offering you what seems to be an interesting and well paying position. If you are interested, you are faced with a decision. Most of us in that situation would probably state the decision something like, "Should I take the new position or stay where I am?" When we view the decision in this manner, however, we actually ignore what may be a much more important and basic decision. If you are interested in an offer of *one particular* job, then the first and basic decision is probably, "Should I change from my present position?" If your decision is yes, then why settle on the single opportunity without first examining others?

Similarly, if you were trying to decide whether to buy a $500 TV, or a $5,000 boat, or a $2,000 tour to Europe, respectively, have you considered the prior question of what is the most satisfying way to spend X amount of money on leisure? Or did you simply take a fancy to one alternative and zero in on that without thinking about other possibilities?

As with helping to change negative feeling states and increasing understanding, there are tools which you can use to help people clarify concerns and learn these decision-making skills.

The desire or need to make a decision is often associated with both a negative feeling state and lack of understanding. Whether it is or is not in a particular instance, needs to be considered. But in the final analysis negative feeling states and lack of understanding only add another dimension to the decision-making process.

Implementing Decisions

The most carefully thought out decision is usually little more than an exercise in futility if satisfactory action does not follow. It is often difficult to separate a decision from the action necessary to implement it. Much of the decision-making process is concerned with thinking through what one must do if a decision is made. Often when we decide not to pursue a course of action it is because of our prediction that we cannot perform the tasks involved. Or, we may not be able to think of a means for putting the decisions into action. In other words, it is often easier for people to decide upon goals than to find ways to pursue them.

Even though it is difficult to completely separate a decision from the action necessary to implement it, people frequently make perfectly reasonable decisions, but simply do not know how to get started, or how to overcome unanticipated obstacles once they are on a course of action. For example, a couple who have decided to repair a marriage, an unskilled worker who decided to acquire skills via a correspondence course, a retired widower deciding to find activities to reduce his boredom, and a college student deciding to engage in activities to counter feelings of loneliness, are all examples of good decisions which may be difficult to implement. But the real payoff in each case comes only with activities which implement the decisions.

Implementing these activities often requires skills and abilities which people may falsely take for granted. For example, Carol and Bill, the couple who decided to repair their marriage, may try to change some of their behavior, such as avoiding name calling and making more positive and caring statements to each other. This sounds easy enough, but can be very difficult because it may seem stilted, self-conscious, and even embarrassing. Making caring statements at times may even be contrary to how they actually feel about each other. In other words, the new desired behavior may not be immediately satisfying. Nevertheless, it is desirable to do it for a period of time until it becomes spontaneous, natural, and sincere, or until they find they can't do it.

But how? There are, for example, two implementation skills which may sustain the behavior until it is satisfying in itself. One is scheduling. That's right; they could program niceness into their relationship. Establish certain times when pleasant comments are to be made. The second relevant implementation skill is reinforcement. Reward, that is, reinforce the performance of the scheduled behavior with pleasant activities such as watching TV, taking a stroll, or making love. It is unlikely, however, that Carol and Bill will think of creating this kind of structure as a means of implementing their decision. A helper in this situation could teach Bill and Carol the skills of scheduling and reinforcment.

Granted, this may not be the typical way you would respond to friends describing (or more likely, complaining about) their marital unhappiness. Let us underscore further, that we are not suggesting that you provide marriage counseling. Rather, as a helper you can suggest ideas which may be difficult to identify by those directly involved in a problem situation.

Similarly, there are ways to help Kelly, the lonely student, implement her decision to become more active. The reason she is lonely in the first place is probably because of lack of information and skills for being more active. She doesn't know how to make things happen for herself. It is hard to imagine many people wanting to be lonely. A helper can provide information and teach Kelly assertiveness and communication skills which will permit her to become socially active; no miracles, just teaching a few ways of taking charge so that she may do what she wants to do.

These four types of helping outcomes cover a wide range of specific changes. We see the four as representing basic solutions to many of life's problems, as well as sources of satisfaction in many areas of life. In nearly all helping situations, the specific outcomes are probably instances of changed feelings, increased understanding, making a decision, and acting on a decision. We will provide many examples of them as we continue.

HELPING TOOLS

In the preceding section, we examined four kinds of outcomes of helping. As noted earlier, helping a person produce the outcomes just described requires that the helper have a variety of helping tools. We have grouped these in four categories:

Basic communication tools

Goal-gaining tools

Behavior observation and description tools

Resource development tools

Following is a brief overview of the kinds of tools you will find in each group. Much of the behavior involved in using the tools will not be new to you. What is different, most likely, is their systematic use as a means of helping others.

Basic Communication Tools

Basic communication tools assist you as helper to (1) communicate acceptance of the people you are helping and (2) help clarify their thinking, feeling, and behaving. Essentially they are tools for "active listening." As contrasted to passive listening, which requires little thought on the part of the listener, "active listening" can be hard work. It requires the listener to pay attention to two levels of communication. An active listener is trying to understand the issues that are being described as well as the *feelings* that the person to whom he is listening has about those issues. The active listener makes predictions about what the speaker is trying to express and then takes some kind of verbal action as a means of helping.

Goal-gaining Tools

Goal-gaining tools are used to help people take specific actions. While the outcomes of using basic communication tools are valuable, people seeking help frequently want more than to change their feeling states and to better understand themselves or a situation. They want help in making more tangible changes. The helper can often provide assistance by using goal-gaining tools such as contracting, reinforcement, modeling, and decision making.

Contracting is an arrangement by which an individual agrees or "contracts" with the helper to do certain activities. One basis of continuing the help becomes a review of how well the contract is being fulfilled. Contracting makes the helping relationship explicit. It eliminates the vagueness—the "maybe I will, maybe I won't"—aspect of many helping situations. In other words, it involves a commitment to engage in specific attempts to bring about desired outcomes.

Modeling and role playing are also goal-gaining tools. They involve trying out new behavior in nonthreatening situations. Consider, for example, the situation of store manager Brown and one of his newly appointed department heads, Ms. Jones. Ms. Jones, an excellent salesperson, found that her attempts to instruct and supervise other salespeople were ineffective. When she offered suggestions and pointed out errors to her staff she frequently got nothing but resentment and hostile reactions in return. Instead of lecturing to her on methods of supervision, Manager Brown "modeled" (acted out) for Ms. Jones different ways of supervising. He actually demonstrated various ways to give verbal feedback to clerks. He then "played the role" of a clerk, and let Ms. Jones role play the things he had demonstrated. Using these two tools he was able to help her obtain her goal of learning better supervisory skills.

Reinforcing (or rewarding) is giving persons support when they take action toward desired outcomes. The reward can take many forms. A child may be given special privileges (such as attending a movie) for cleaning his or her room, or a secretary may be given opportunities to attend management workshops if there is improved performance of regularly assigned responsibilities. The continuance of providing help, itself, also can be used as a reward.

There are several tools useful for helping people make decisions. These include helping people define their objectives, identify alternative means for achieving goals, and develop procedures for analyzing risks and predicting needed resources.

Behavior Observation and Description Tools

The tools in this category are essentially methods for *observing* and *describing behavior*. In situations where a group has a concern or problem, an outsider or at least relatively impartial observer can be effective. To the extent that the observers are neutral and objective, they can help a group focus on facts and information instead of getting entangled in bias, opinions, and selective perceptions. Everything from office squabbles to family arguments often happen when people have different understandings and perceptions of the meaning of their own and others' behavior. Not infrequently people begin to evaluate before they describe. Describing what is happening in a group, however, can be a difficult task. There are a number of concepts and procedures for observing and describing behavior that help people better understand the dynamics of their interactions.

Resource Development Tools

The tools in this group are used to identify resources and make them more available to people who need them. In the long run these tools may be the most useful ones you as a lay helper can develop. They consist largely of getting information to people, establishing sources of help for specific problems, and facilitating the uses of resources. We describe agencies and provide annotated lists of information sources regarding several topics about which people frequently seek help. The lists are not exhaustive, but they can serve as a basic reference for people in helping roles. This section also describes ways of identifying potential resources in a community. A means of getting people in touch with resources is also described.

HELPING STRATEGIES

How do you as a helper put it all together? How can the helping tools be used to assist people to achieve desired outcomes? Strategy, in a word, is the name of the game. Strategies are means, ways, or plans for using helping tools. One of the most challenging aspects of helping is developing effective strategies. When should active listening be used? When and how to best present information? How to most effectively motivate a child to try a new activity? How best to help a bashful person gain self-confidence? How and under what circumstances to best confront a person with negative behavior observations?

Developing effective strategies requires imagination, sensitivity, and good perceptual abilities. Lest we mislead you, it should be said that we are not referring to master plans associated with war games or national sales campaigns. The strategies pertinent to the kinds of help with which you as helper are concerned are relatively straightforward. Know why you are using particular helping tools at a particular time. What is *your* purpose? Are you doing active listening as a means for aiding self-understanding, reducing anger, or establishing a relationship? Those are examples of strategy. By way of contrast, if you are listening to someone complain simply because you can't think of any other way to respond, then you are without a strategy. In addition to enhancing your helping efforts and making better use of your time, strategies can keep you out of a whole lot of trouble which can otherwise develop from haphazard attempts to be helpful. Two chapters are devoted to developing helping strategies.

SUMMARY

In this chapter we have described the helping process as one which assists people as they change from a state of "things are not as I want them to be," to a state of "things are more like I want them to be." Changes are brought about in part by helpers using helping tools in a purposeful, considered manner. Several outcomes of helping and four kinds of helping tools were described briefly. With this as an overview, we move in the next chapter to a consideration of personal characteristics of effective helpers and an examination of important aspects of the helping relationship.

EXERCISES

1 To make you more aware of the variety of helping relationships you have in your life, list all of the people you currently consider to be your significant helpers and then describe the kind of assistance they give you.

HELPER	KIND OF ASSISTANCE RECEIVED

Now list all of the people to whom you give significant help and describe the kind of assistance you give.

PERSON HELPED	KIND OF ASSISTANCE GIVEN

Are you surprised at the number of people you listed? Was it difficult to describe the kind of assistance given or received? If so, think in terms of helping outcomes (pp. 9–16).

2 In order to get a better understanding of the kinds of outcomes the people in your life tend to seek, do the following. First, list the names of important others in your life (family, friends, coworkers) in the left-hand column of the following chart. Then think about the last few times you have helped these people. Then indicate by a check mark (x) which helping outcome each person usually sought.

What did you discover? Sometimes you find that persons always come to you when they are blue and hope that you will help them change their feeling state. Perhaps your child always seeks you out when trying to make a decision. Reviewing this chart can make you more aware of what helping tools are most important for you to learn.

IMPORTANT OTHERS	HELPING OUTCOMES				
	Change in Feeling State	Increased Understanding	Decisions	Implementing Decisions	

3 We are going to encourage you to keep a journal (a steno pad or blank book would be appropriate) while you're reading and practicing this book. To begin your journal, write your current definition of helping. What does helping mean to you? Perhaps a list of words or phrases instead of complete sentences would do. We will come back to your definition of helping later.

Write the following headings at the top of the first page of your journal. Then each day record in your journal specific helping situations.

PERSON HELPED AND SITUATION	OUTCOME THEY WANTED	HELPING ACTIVITY	EFFECT OF HELPING

We encourage you to start this now even though you haven't learned about helping tools and strategies so that you can develop a clearer idea of the kind of helper you are currently. Starting now will also give you a record of progress in improving your helping skills.

Three | Personal Characteristics of Helpers

Your personality is a very important part of the helping process. By personality we mean both the way in which you come across to people and specific characteristics such as honesty, warmth, sincerity, and confidence. Regardless of the helping tools you possess, the effect of your personality on others is a crucial part of the helping process. The purpose of the first part of this chapter is to help you review some of your personal characteristics and consider their effect on your helping efforts.

Nearly all helping takes place within the context of some basic relationship. In any given helping situation, you are first of all a father, mother, friend, supervisor, or member of some other basic relationship. The basic relationship between you and the person you are helping affects your attempts to be helpful. Too often important conditions in a helping situation become apparent only after the helper has become entangled in the life of another person in a way that may be both unpleasant for the helper, and not very helpful for the person wanting help. Some of these conditions can be anticipated and dealt with once their potential occurrence is recognized. Examining a means for assessing five dimensions of basic relationships is the purpose of the second part of this chapter.

SOME GENERALLY POSITIVE CHARACTERISTICS

Some helper personality characteristics that enhance helping relationships include warmth, honesty, sincerity, acceptance, perceptiveness, self-confidence, openness, and interest in other people. Can you express a genuine interest in other people? Can you listen to others express values contrary to your own without feeling defensive, or resentful? Do you usually "get the point" of what others say? When you don't understand, are you able to identify what is confusing you? Can you empathize with other people, that is, understand their feelings without feeling sorry for them? Can you listen to accounts of unfair and dishonest behavior without being shocked (or at least not revealing your shock)? Can you often see some humor in generally agonizing or stupid situations? Do you usually refrain from giving unwanted or unasked-for advice? Can you accept ways of doing a task different from your own? Can you deal with unpleasant tasks without becoming emotionally unstrung? Are you able to communicate your displeasure regarding another person's behavior without becoming unpleasant yourself? Can you assert yourself without offending others, or at least not be upset if they are offended?

If you can give positive answers to most of these questions, you are likely a person who is potentially an effective helper. An effective helper is more often than not reasonably objective, self-confident and is a person who has developed purpose and direction in many areas of his or her own life. In addition, effective helpers are probably aware of and sensitive to how people react to them.

THE OTHER SIDE OF THE COIN

Now let's look at some personal characteristics which may inhibit helping. Do you have a set of rigid values by which you tend to judge others? Do you usually see other people pretty much as types, instead of seeing them as many-sided? Do you take sides quickly? When you listen, are you anxious for the other person to finish so you can make your point? Is it difficult for you to keep another's confidence? Do you tend to become preoccupied with another person's problems as if they were your own? Are you easily upset? Do you usually want to react immediately to a small, but annoying emotional situation? Are you uncomfortable when you must deal with more than a few things at a time? If you answer yes to most of these questions, then think through carefully the impressions you make on people wanting help.

Another way to assess your potential for helping is to compare your own helping behavior with those of several types of would-be helpers. We have noted four of them below. Obviously, they are caricatures, but most of us have experienced them at one time or another.

One of the most irritating would-be helpers is the "You
think you've got a problem! Let me tell you about mine"
type. With some exceptions, personal concerns of the
helper have no place in the helping relationship. Bob,
for example, wants to unload his woes regarding his no-
good boss and some company policies he thinks are idi-
otic. His friend, Dan, rather than hearing him out,
continually interjects complaints about his own job
situation. Dan appears to be oblivious to Bob's concerns
and would not be an effective helper. His responses have
nothing to do with Bob's concerns. If you are at a time
in your life when preoccupations with your own concerns keep you from paying attention to those of others,
then it is probably not wise to enter a helping relationship.

Another would-be helper is the "Let me tell you what
to do" type. For example, a physician, after treating a
woman patient, listens to her complain about her teenage daughter's sloppy habits around the house, and her
unsuccessful efforts to get the girl to "shape up." The
physician advises the mother to lay down certain rules
for the daughter, stipulate the punishments for not following them, and then enforce them.

"You've simply got to be firm with the girl," he says.
"Tell her what you expect, and let the chips fall where
they may."

The physician was advising the mother to apply
a principle which says that people learn when they experience the consequences of their actions. While a useful principle, it was of little help to the mother. Some of
the possible consequences of using this "do as I say" approach for the family of a fifteen-year-old girl could be
far more serious than the present situation. The mother
presently is dealing with a messy room and cleaning up
after her daughter. If she follows the simplistic advice
of the physician she may have resentment, lying, and
increased uncooperativeness on her hands. In order to
be helpful, the physician could have explained the
principle to her, helped her think through potential
negative outcomes of using it, and suggested specific

ways of implementing it. For example, it would be important to inform and gain the support of the father and other members of the family regarding the "new rules." People who offer ready-made simple solutions often do a disservice. If they lack the time and/or patience to help others understand how to use their suggestions, they probably ought not offer them in the first place.

I'll take charge. In most situations the effective helper is not the person who "takes charge." (Of course there are exceptions, usually situations involving an emergency or crisis.) For example, when Mr. Jones loses control of his first grade class, his principal, Ms. Apple, may "take charge," but probably for a brief period. Ms. Apple's more important help will be the supervision she provides Mr. Jones over the next few months while he learns classroom management skills. The effective helper views another person's problem as just that, the other person's problem. A simple truth is involved. Namely, when you take on the responsibility for solving another person's problem it's no longer just that person's problem; it becomes yours. You may solve it this time, but what about next time?

Examples of the "take charge" approach to helping occur every day in many job and family situations. A secretary goes to her boss and complains that a coworker is not cooperating. The boss' response is, "Let me talk with Martha and I think I can clear up the difficulty."

A mother tells her husband about a disagreement she has had with one of their children. The husband's "help" is to say, "I'll have a talk with the kid and straighten things out."

What effect did the "helpers" have in either case? While they may have smoothed over problems, they also "taught" the persons seeking help that the way to deal with subsequent problems is to get someone else to assume responsibility for solving them. The "take charge" approach may appear to save time for the helper, but it does little in the long run for the person wanting help. Most of the time no one can solve our problems for us. Each individual must assume the responsibility for his or her own behavior according to his or her level of maturity. The helper can assist the individual do what that person wants to do—but the individual must do it.

I once had the problem myself. Another would-be helper is the "I understand because I once had the problem myself" person. Believing he or she has resolved a problem, he or she is eager to make newfound insights available to others with the same "problem." Carol is an example of this sort of helper. Carol is a popular and outgoing woman who had recently gone through a divorce. She believed that she understood very well the circumstances leading to her divorce. Actually she was ignorant of many of the circumstances, primarily because she and her ex-husband had seldom been frank with each other about their concerns. Several of her female friends sought her out for help regarding their own marital problems. Believing she had successfully dealt with her own, Carol suggested that her friends adopt the solution she had used. Her solution, of course, was extremely inappropriate for some of her friends. Their problems were very different from hers.

One of the shortcomings of the "I had the problem myself" helpers is that they tend to think and react in terms of labels, ignoring the fact that the same label can have many different meanings. It is clear that "My kid is disobedient," or "My wife is frigid," or "I'm unhappy with my job," or "My father doesn't understand me," each has a multitude of possible meanings. They are general labels. To respond in essence by saying, "Aha! I know your problem; let me tell you what I did," is usually not very helpful.

You may have erroneously concluded by now that all effective helpers are warm, sincere, supersensitive saints. That is not true. Most of us probably have experienced the Dutch uncle, or the hard, confronting boss, or the tough, demanding and directive teacher, or the "I'm going to straighten you out right now" parent. There is no question that such people can be helpful. Chances are that these people possessed some of the positive attributes discussed earlier. Your tough, but helpful father was most likely genuinely concerned with your well-being and somehow communicated this to you. The confronting boss who made you feel inadequate and guilty for the moment, but who helped you, was probably sincere and fair. Sometimes, in other words, people are able to provide help in spite of certain personal attributes.

To recognize that some people are more helpful than others is not to say that there is a single best type of helping personality. The concept of an ideal helping personality, that is, a certain combination of personality characteristics which is more help-producing than any other combinations, is a myth. When we ask questions such as: Helpful to whom? For what purpose? Under what conditions? common sense indicates that a great variety of "personality types" can be helpful. And some people, helpful in one situation, are useless in others. The warm, kindly, gentle pastor of a rural parish who is very helpful to the church members he has known most of his life may be totally ineffective as a helping resource when transferred to a central-city parish. The style and manner of a retired Lt. Colonel who was sought out by many soldiers for his understanding and positive direction, may be unacceptable to students as an adviser at a liberal arts college.

There is simply no superhelper type. It is even misleading to assume that what are commonly thought of as positive personal characteristics always enhance helping. Very shy people, for example, can be frightened by warm, outgoing, enthusiastic helpers. (So can some not so shy people, for that matter). The opposite is also true. We have observed people who are retiring nearly to the point of being withdrawn, who are very helpful to some people.

Nevertheless, there are certain personality attributes which appear to increase the probabilities that one can be helpful to a wide range of people. Likewise, there are other personality characteristics which in most instances inhibit being helpful. We have noted some of both, not for purposes of providing a prescription for a helping personality, but to assist you to consider how your personality affects your attempts to help. An accurate and honest assessment of "how you come across" to others can provide a basis for deciding which kinds of helping tools are most suitable for you to use.

BASIC RELATIONSHIPS AND HELPING

We don't help in a vacuum. There is always a basic relationship between you and the person you are helping and those relationships influence your helping efforts. It is wise to be aware of them. Basic relationships vary in both intensity and complexity. At one extreme would be stranger-stranger and volunteer—shut-in relationships, and at the other, parent-child and husband-wife relationships. Other basic relationships, such as teacher-student, supervisor-employee, police-citizen, guard-prisoner, nurse-patient, professional practitioner-client, have varying intensity and complexity. The important thing to remember about basic relationships is that they are the context within which helping takes place. If you are trying to help Jill make a decision about having a child, for example, the nature of your help will be determined in part by your basic relationship with her. It will differ, for example, depending upon whether you are a friend of the same sex, lover, spouse, parent, offspring, supervisor, or physician. Each of these relationships probably involves some unique values and concerns. In one relationship you may be charging Jill a fee for helping, in another you may be representing an agency or some organization, and in yet another you may have a legal responsibility for Jill. Whether seen as constraints or advantages, the conditions of these basic relationships affect your helping.

Clearly then, important considerations of helping include the values and conditions of basic relationships. These are often so critically important that they preclude attempting to offer help. You may have such strong opinions about what a person should or shouldn't do that objective helping may be near impossible. There may be certain issues about which a spouse can't help a mate, a parent its child, a lover its companion, or a friend a friend. Basic relationships must be considered when help is to be offered.

Rather than examine all possible basic relationships, let's examine five relationship dimensions. These dimensions can serve as a checklist for analyzing any particular relationship within which you are contemplating helping. The five relationship dimensions, in regard to helping, are (1) authority, (2) confidentiality, (3) commitment, (4) psychological closeness, and (5) dependency. Let's examine each.

Authority

In many helping situations one person appears to have authority over another. The two people are usually associated on some basis which underlies the need for specific help. Both people anticipate that the basic relationship will continue after the helping situation has passed. Authority relationships include parent-child, teacher-student, and employer-employee. Examples of other relationships which have at least implications of authority are physician-patient, nurse-patient, other professional people such as attorneys and architects and their clients, and a variety of adult-child supervisory relationships.

The validity of the concept of absolute authority is questionable, that is, how often can one person really "make" another do something against his or her will? Nevertheless, authority in the sense of a powerful influence of one person over another is real.

When authority exists in a relationship, it can conflict with the freedom to reject help. For example, a friend-friend relationship has no implications for authority. Consequently, the friend is under no compulsion to accept the help or bend to the wishes of the friend-helper. In a supervisor-employee relationship, in contrast, there is an element of authority, and the worker is not free to ignore the help of the supervisor in regard to work matters.

An obvious example of the authority-helping conflict is a parent-child situation. Father says to his sixteen-year-old son, Bill, "I don't want you to quit school, but the decision is yours. Whatever you do, I would like to help you think it through." Chances are that he doesn't mean just that. What the father probably means is that he will not use his authority if Bill decides to stay in school, but will attempt to use it if Bill decides to quit. The fact that Bill knows this, limits the help his father can provide.

This is not to suggest that helping cannot occur within an authority relationship. Obviously, it does and frequently. Nevertheless, well-intentioned efforts to help often fall flat because either the helper, or person being helped, or both don't recognize the limits which the authority imposes on helping. Recognizing those limits before proceeding is one means of reducing the handicap.

In the previous example, father might have said, "Bill, you know that I'm going to urge you to continue school, to do everything I can to see that you do. But, I also realize that forcing you into something against your will wouldn't be very good either. Let's face it. If you feel strongly enough about it, I really cannot force you. But I would like to help if possible. Can we put aside the business of our disagreement and look at the situation? Maybe it doesn't have to be go or no go. Perhaps we can find alternatives." Bill may tell his father to "Go to hell—you wouldn't understand anyway!" But, on the basis of his father leveling with him regarding authority, Bill may talk it over, and help has started.

Implied in this example is a principle regarding authority in a helping relationship. Simply stated, it is: recognize and deal directly with the authority aspect of the relationship if it appears to be getting in your way. You need to decide upon the nature and extent of the authority. How real is it? What would be the possible consequences of using or enforcing authority? After asking such questions, you can come to several conclusions. At one extreme, you can attempt to enforce the authority and abandon any attempt to help. Or, all parties involved can recognize the handicaps imposed by the authority and attempt to work within them. Finally, one can decide to forego any attempt to enforce authority, hoping that this will clear the way for helping, and live with the consequences. None of these may be entirely satisfactory, but they are better than ignoring an authority aspect of a relationship when it interferes with helping.

Confidentiality

As a helper, people often tell you things they consider confidential. The individual does not want you to reveal what is told to you. Because of the complexity of many helping relationships, this can put the helper in a bind.

Gloria, a neighbor, tells you she plans to run away from home, and wants to air her concerns with you. Can you keep her confidence, or do you believe you must tell her parents?

Steve, a fellow employee, discovers that one of the supervisors is stealing from the company. Steve is trying to decide what to do with his information. Should he tell the manager, confront the supervisor, or do nothing? Steve wants your help in thinking through the alternatives. He decides, after talking with you, to do nothing. Steve appears to be the only one in the company who has direct knowledge or proof of the situation. Thus, if you inform the manager about the situation, you would of necessity involve Steve. What do you do? Which is more important: maintaining Steve's confidence, or your responsibility to the company?

Candi talks to one of her teachers in confidence about hard drugs being pushed at school, and reveals a source. Should the teacher break Candi's confidence and inform the school principal?

There is no simple answer to the question of confidentiality, but it is one which helpers must resolve from time to time. In the final anaysis, the resolution is always a value judgment. One approach to resolving the problem of confidentiality is to deal with it directly. In many instances, it is possible to raise the issue with people you are helping prior to their revealing confidential information to you. For example, if Gloria had come to you about feeling an urge to run away from home, you might have said:

> Gloria, I'm willing to listen, but let's decide between us how confidential this conversation is going to be. What do you expect me to do with what you may tell me, and what do you expect me not to do?

In some situations you may decide not to become involved in a helping relationship because you have serious doubts about your willingness to keep the other person's confidence. That may seem a little harsh. Wouldn't it be disappointing to say to someone asking for help, "I'm sorry, but under those conditions I won't become involved." It probably would, but in contrast to the potential harm done by breaking a confidence, it is less destructive. Remember, you can't be helpful to everyone. Even if you have the skills, time, interest, and emotional strength required, sometimes you may not be willing to respect a requested confidence, or be unable to predict whether or not you can.

Commitment

Before engaging in a helping relationship, consider the extent of commitment you are willing to make to the other person. Sometimes you may not want or be able to devote the amount of time you predict would be necessary to help another person. A supervisor may have time to help a worker sort out some personal concerns once in awhile, but probably doesn't want to meet with the person two or three times a week for several months.

Some attempts to be helpful may require more energy and psychological commitment than you are willing to give. Imagine a married couple, both very good friends of yours, who indicate that they have serious marital problems. Since you know them both, and because they think you can be an objective listener, they ask you to listen to a description of their differences and provide them with an objective evaluation. Imagine further that you already understand certain aspects of the situation. To be more explicit, you know that both have had extramarital affairs unknown to one another. You value both of their friendships. Do you really want to become entangled? You predict that the role of listener and arbitrator will be draining and unpleasant. Are you willing to try to be helpful in view of the unpleasantness? You may or may not decide to make the commitment. The important consideration is to know what is involved.

Being inattentive or unrealistic about what you are willing to commit to helping someone can lead to trouble. Accusations of, "You really don't care about me," and all kinds of unproductive but predictable and unnecessary unpleasantness can result. The time to be realistic about commitments is at the beginning of helping. The claim that helping is like being pregnant—there are no degrees—is simply not true. You can offer varying amounts of help. It is you who must determine the commitment, and in some cases explain why you are setting limits on it.

Psychological Closeness

All of us have experienced situations in which we wanted to assist someone but felt that we were too close to be helpful. It is a different consideration from commitment. When you evaluate the extent of your commitment, you believe that you could be helpful but question whether you want to take or have the time or energy needed. "Being too close" refers to a situation in which you believe that some aspect of your relationship with the other person would prevent you from being helpful. It may mean that you have feelings about the other person which could prohibit you from seeing things from their point of view or from being objective. The feelings may be negative, such as resentment and anger, or positive such as love and respect. The feelings may inhibit helping under some circumstances and make little or no difference in another. For example, Sally and Jane are sisters-in-law. Sally's husband earns considerably more than Jane's, and Jane is resentful. Jane is a good listener and over the years has helped Sally clarify a number of confusing personal issues. However, Jane is aware that when she listens to Sally talk about financial concerns, her resentment pops up and she ceases to be helpful to Sally. Recognizing this, Jane explains her inability to listen to Sally's financial concerns, but says she is willing to listen and attempt to help with other issues.

"Being too close" to another person can also mean that one or both of you is incapable of perceiving the other accurately in a given situation. For example, Sue finds that her efficiency at the office often results in poor relations with some of her coworkers. She is a person who, when she sees something that needs to be done, does it quickly and effectively. She finds, however, that sometimes her coworkers resent her efficiency and interpret her as being pushy, overly aggressive, and presumptuous. She is upset and turns to Harry, her husband, for clarification. Sue's efficiency, however, is viewed by Harry as one of her great strengths. It is a characteristic of hers for which he has a great deal of admiration, and he cannot understand anyone else resenting it. Consequently, he assures her that her coworkers must be wrong. In this instance, Sue would do better by turning to someone more "objective" for help.

Some kinds of psychologically close relationships are extremely complex, and require the two people involved to deal with a great many issues and mutual concerns. In a marriage relationship, for example, one person may have opinions and beliefs that the partner cannot understand or tolerate. Trying to help one another when such a difference exists could be futile. Consider Marge and Bob. Their children are now grown. Marge wants to devote her energies to volunteer work. She is especially interested in working with elderly people. She and Bob have discussed her interests and plans many times. Bob has stated that he thinks working with older people would be a mistake. In his opinion there are many more important community needs. He is sure that Marge will become discouraged and upset over the conditions she will discover and frustrated about not having an impact on changing them. And he "knows" she does not deal effectively with frustration. Both of their positions are clear, and they feel strongly about them. Marge pursues her interests and becomes actively involved in programs for the elderly. Soon she experiences the frustration that Bob predicted. Nevertheless she is committed to continuing her work. She also wants to talk with someone to clarify her concerns.

Usually Bob would be an appropriate person to turn to for help, but not in this instance. Rightly or wrongly, he feels strongly that his wife ought not be involved in the program for the elderly, and it infuriates him when she complains about her concerns. He "knows" that this is not an appropriate activity for her. He is too close to be objective, and would be wise to tell her so, suggesting that she find someone else to help with this particular issue.

When psychological closeness appears to hamper an attempt to help, it is useful to acknowledge it. We can then attempt to assist the other person to understand why we feel too close to be helpful and perhaps identify someone else who may be a more appropriate source of help.

Dependency

What is a dependency relationship? It's a relationship in which one person believes they must involve another in major decisions and problems. There's nothing mysterious about such relationships, or how they develop. They are learned. If, for example, a wife assists her husband in resolving a conflict with a child, the husband probably observes that she is helpful. Let's say that this happens several times, that is, the husband and child have conflicts, the husband asks for (or the wife simply offers) help, and the conflict is resolved. The husband in this situation can learn two things. He can observe and learn what the wife does to resolve the conflicts. He can then try to use the same procedure on his own. If it is effective, then there is no need to involve the wife in future conflicts. Or, he can learn that the best way to resolve conflicts with children is to continue to involve the wife. Ultimately, such involvement can become a nuisance for the wife. She now has acquired responsibility for a parent-child relationship problem which was initially that of her husband. The husband learned to lean on his wife. By regularly solving the father-child conflicts for him, she taught him to be dependent.

Obviously, many healthy relationships involve being able to rely on another for help. When we speak of dependent relationships, we are not referring to this positive aspect of relationships. The reference in dependent relationships is to excessive dependencies which debilitate the people involved.

Most textbooks about counseling and psychotherapy caution against fostering dependency relationships. The same warning applies to the kind of helping relationships with which we are concerned here. We touched the idea when we described the "take charge" helper. The idea is so important that we will repeat it: dependency relationships are "no-nos."

Nearly all kinds of significant relationships have the potential for developing dependencies. Excluding situations where helping is a one-shot deal, helpers may well have two purposes. The first is to provide assistance with whatever issue is involved. The second is to assist others to develop self-reliance so that they will have less need for help in the future. In the previous example, for instance, the wife could have explained what she was doing to resolve conflicts and why, thus assisting the husband to learn new skills rather than becoming dependent upon her.

Volunteer helpers in agencies and institutions often have experience with people who seek out relationships that allow for dependency. That is understandable. People want attention, friends and companionship, and when these are difficult to obtain in positive ways, resorting to trapping the helper into providing them is not surprising. Temporarily, the dependencies may even be appealing to helpers, especially if the helper depends for gratification on helping others. It can be nice to be wanted; rewarding to be asked for help. But in the end the dependent relationship serves no one well. Those being helped come to be resented and usually do not develop the skills which enhance the free living of their own lives. The helpers become restricted and burdened with the problems of others, thus also limiting their freedom.

All of these relationship conditions—authority, confidentiality, commitment, psychological closeness, and dependency—are important. We suggest that one approach to resolving them when they exist is to deal with them openly and directly. To many of us, such frankness seems somewhat unnatural or at least difficult. We hesitate to deal directly because we fear personal or social embarrassment. One reason for the embarrassment is that people often lack the interpersonal skills to be open without also being obnoxious. One goal of the remainder of this book is to help you learn skills for dealing openly and effectively with potentially difficult helping situations.

SUMMARY

Two sets of conditions can affect the outcomes of your attempts to help: your personality, and the nature of the basic relationship between you and the person wanting help. Giving some thought to the implications of the possible constraints on offering help which have been described can give direction regarding how and to what extent you are willing to become involved in helping others. In some instances, you may conclude that your potential as a helper is negligible, or that the risks of trying to help are greater than you want to take. We have urged you to deal directly with these conditions when they exist. Be careful how you become involved in other peoples' lives, for your own well-being as well as theirs.

A POINT OF VIEW

We want to acknowledge our personal point of view about our concept of helping. Our concept of helping reflects a particular philosophical perspective. We could have noted this earlier, but it will make more sense to you after reading these first chapters. If labels are useful, our view includes both humanistic and behavioral perspectives. It is humanistic because it embraces the idea that most people will be happier if they are nice to each other. It focuses on behavior in that it assumes that being nice to each other requires certain concepts and skills which many people don't learn in the natural turn of events. It also involves a certain sense of democracy by suggesting that the person being helped should desire change and share in the decision to accept help. There are other philosophical approaches which would preclude helping or offer it under quite a different set of assumptions. For example, one could propose an approach involving authoritarian helpers and a set of absolute values.

While humanistic and valuing niceness, our position also includes the belief that the world can be a pretty tough place; that it has a good deal of unhappiness, dissatisfaction, and misery. But while acknowledging the great imperfections of the human race, we believe most of the responsibility for people's problems rests with people. Certainly, chance runs rampant—falling safes, speeding trains, wars, and all of that. But satisfaction is much more a function of what you do about yourself than what others might do for you. And that's when helping is important; when one has taken responsibility for one's own development and well-being, the assistance of another is most useful. Finally, from all of this, it should be clear that not everyone can be helpful or be helped all of the time.

That's the point of view from which we write.

EXERCISES

1   How do you come across? You might make a list of all of the terms you can think of which describe your personality. If you have the courage, ask a friend, a boss, a child, a spouse, a roommate, a coworker or whoever you think appropriate to read the list and check those items which they agree describe you. Ask them to add others to the list if they can. If the check marks are few, you may want to compare your self-description with someone you trust and can talk with easily. But remember, don't be defensive and don't argue. The outcome you are seeking, if this suggestion appeals to you, is simply to obtain a better understanding of how others see you.

2 If you want to get the feedback, ask five people you have helped recently to write a short statement about your positive helping characteristics. Then ask an objective friend to read the statements and discuss with the friend the following:

Do the statements agree on some characteristics?

Do the statements agree with your perceptions of yourself?

3 At the top of each column below, list a person whom you often seek out when you need help. Below each name, list the characteristics these people have that, in your opinion, make them effective helpers.

#1	#2	#3

Look at your lists. What do they tell you about helping characteristics, in general; and, more specifically, what does the list tell you about your needs and values when seeking help?

4   Consider for a minute the different helping relationships in your life. In how many of these relationships do you have some authority over the other person (e.g., parent, boss, older relative, higher status)? List four of these relationships in the first column. In the second briefly describe the last time you helped this person. Then in the third column note how, if at all, your helping would have been different if you did not have "authority" over the other person.

RELATIONSHIP (Example: Father-Daughter)	LAST HELPING SITUATION WITH PERSON	Describe how helping might have differed if the person was not under your authority.

From looking at your response in column 3, estimate the impact authority really has in your helping relationships. Is it a great deal or not? If it is a great deal in some relationships, does your "authority" make you less effective?

5   Reread pages 25–27 which describe ineffective helpers. Then rate yourself on the following scale by checking the boxes which best describe how often you behave in a way similar to each of the four types.

INEFFECTIVE HELPER TYPE	Very Often	Occasionally	Not Guilty
"You think you got a problem. Let me tell you mine!"			
"If you would just do what I say . . ."			
"Let me take charge."			
"I understand because I once had the problem myself."			

Your Rating

How do you fare? If you have four marks in the first column, you have some work ahead of you to become an effective helper. In your journal write down each of the ineffective helper types and make a tally each time you find you were an ineffective helper. Try to decrease the tallies weekly.

Four | Basic Helping Tools

ACTIVE LISTENING

Helping begins with communication. Someone is describing a problem, relating a concern, expressing troublesome feelings, or in some manner trying to communicate how life is not as he or she wants it to be. You begin most instances of helping by listening. This chapter describes and illustrates some basic communication tools designed to help you do active listening.

Why *active* listening? Isn't listening, listening? Not really. We listen for different purposes and with varying amounts of attention. In some arguments, for example, our listening often concentrates on discovering weak points in the other person's case. We may not be interested in understanding what they have to say. Listening to small talk at parties may be minimally intense because of our preoccupation with moving through the room full of people to meet a friend. In many conversations our main purpose in listening is to discover when we can begin talking. Listening as noted in the examples is essentially done for personal reasons.

Active listening, in contrast, is used in helping situations as a means of assisting the people you are helping. What you learn from active listening is not its primary purpose. The act of listening itself and what you do with what you learn is what is most important. Active listening is a means of assisting people clarify thoughts and feelings, and to increase their understanding of self, others, and circumstances.

Active listening is purposeful and considered. It is intended to have helpful outcomes for the person you are assisting. It is also hard work. Active listening involves trying to understand what the other person is thinking and why. It requires developing empathy with their feelings, avoiding pity for their circumstances, and being nonevaluative of their behavior. When you do active listening, you are saying to the other person:

I accept you as you are. I'm trying to understand your concerns and empathize with your feelings. I'm interested in you. I'm attempting to avoid evaluating your thoughts and actions. I may or may not agree with them, but in this situation my opinions are irrelevant. My purpose is to help you develop useful feelings and understandings about yourself.

Active listening tools are useful in many helping situations. They are basic. Without them a helper will find it difficult to use the goal-gaining, behavior description, and resource development tools discussed in the following chapters. In this chapter, however, the concern is with using the basic tools by themselves.

The effective use of active listening tools can have several outcomes including: alleviating a general sense of aloneness, changing specific feeling states, relieving tension, revealing sources of confusion and uncertainty, promoting self-understanding, and motivating decisions and planning.

Why is active listening an effective helping tool? How does it contribute to the outcomes just noted? Consider loneliness as an example. Feeling alone in the world with one's concerns can be a painful and debilitating experience. How does active listening help alleviate aloneness? When you listen to another's concerns, you are in effect acknowledging the importance of those concerns as well as the other person. That individual now knows that at least one other person believes those concerns are important enough to warrant attention. Someone cares. An awareness that someone else knows and cares about those concerns can lessen the preoccupation with one's problem per se, and thus free some energy for considering solutions. Thus, active listening is a means of demonstrating interest and concern.

Using listening to change specific feeling states is a common occurrence. Having someone listen to you blowing off steam can quickly reduce your anger and frustration. Listening, as most of us have experienced or observed, can even reverse another person's feeling states. Consider, for example, the person who comes to you angrily shouting about a situation and leaves five minutes later laughing over the absurdity of it all. Listening helps change feelings by providing people with the opportunity to "hear themselves" and reevaluate the seriousness and reasonableness of their feelings.

People like others to listen to them. There is a story which went around several years back about a woman selling psychotherapy. It seems that in spite of a busy practice she lacked whatever degrees or licenses those who regulate such things believed she should have. She was told, consequently, that she could no longer advertise or sell psychotherapy. She would be in legal trouble if she continued. Having grown accustomed to living the life style of a full-time psychotherapist, she was obviously displeased. Her solution, according to the story, was simple and effective. She took down her psychotherapy sign and had a new one painted. It reads *Listening*. Apparently, she is doing very well.

Listening reduces tension. While some psychological tension can serve as a positive motivation to action, extreme tension has negative effects on most of us. In general, when we are tense we are less likely to cope with people and difficult situations. Because tension is frequently caused by a situation or individual with whom we must continue to deal, it often has a spiraling effect on us. For example, a pupil is tense about poor relations with a teacher. The student tries to deal with the situation while under tension. Because of tension, the pupil is even less effective, which increases the tension, and on and on. Talking with someone else about a tense situation, that is, being listened to, often diffuses the tension and allows effective coping to take over.

Verbalizing one's concerns to someone else can also result in understanding more clearly the source of confusion, the specific causes of concern, or the reasons why you are reacting as you are. As we will demonstrate, active listening is an important aspect of many helping efforts.

TOOLS FOR ACTIVE LISTENING

Passive listening in its purest form would involve your sitting like a toad on a leaf offering no response to what is being said. In that sense, passive listening is rare. Most people, when listening, make some response to what is being said. Nevertheless, a good deal of listening is passive in the sense that the listener's responses are made without much purpose. They are more or less spontaneous reactions. In other words, in passive listening the listener is not purposefully concerned with the outcome of listening.

Active listening, in contrast, is concerned with the outcomes of the act of listening. The active listener is aware of his or her own reactions and knows that he or she is attempting to help the other person. Let's illustrate. Imagine a friend says something like the following to you:

> Wow! I've had it. The job is not going well, the kids aren't helping at home and Jeff isn't interested in my problems. Something's got to give. I'm about to climb the walls. Know what I mean? I mean I've got to get away for awhile—even a weekend. I don't understand why everything falls in on me at once! Why can't Jeff and the kids take some of the pressure off me at home? Then, maybe I could square things up at work. What do you think?

After listening to this, how would you respond? Following are some nonactive listening thoughts and responses. (Thoughts are given first in brackets; responses follow in quotations.)

[She's off again!] "They really are unfair."

[I've got to get home soon.] "Yeah, but things will get better."

[I wish she would shut up.] "My Harry is the same way; let me tell you about last Saturday night. . . ."

Listening responses such as these are not necessarily inappropriate. They may be. But they do not illustrate active listening. Examples of active listening thoughts and responses are:

[She is upset.] "You're upset."

[She is upset and may want to talk through the problem.] "You seem upset . . . would it help to talk about what's bothering you? I'm willing to listen."

[What are her major concerns? I can't tell and I doubt that she understands.] "I believe you're upset, but I'm not sure about the causes. Do you want some help in sorting out the family and job concerns?"

Further, the listener can be specific about the intended effect the reactions will have on the speaker. The listener can do this because he or she is using relatively specific listening tools. Three of these tools are: *acceptance, clarification,* and *probing*.

Acceptance

One of the basic listening tools is the ability to communicate acceptance of another person. The message of acceptance is essentially, "I hear you, I'm interested in you and what you are saying, and your need to say it. Further, I'm trying not to make any value judgments about you, or what you are saying."

The message of acceptance can be stated to the other person directly, in just so many words. While sometimes appropriate, a formal statement of acceptance often seems stilted. There are other ways of communicating acceptance. These include smiling, nodding one's head, and making brief comments such as, "I see," "Yes, that's important to you," "Go on," or "It's difficult to discuss isn't it?" The following excerpt from a conversation illustrates communicating acceptance. In the illustration, a mother is talking to a friend about her strained relationship with her teenage daughter:

"She resents everything I try to do for her. Why, I don't know. When she doesn't clean her room, I do it for her. When she forgets to iron a blouse I do it. But all I ever get in return is crassness—she doesn't thank me—she's even sullen and resentful. But then I shouldn't burden you with all this!"

"I'm interested," replied the friend. "It does bother you."

"It sure does. It's getting worse and worse," the mother continued. "I thought it was a stage she was going through, but the older she gets the worse she gets."

"It's discouraging," acknowledged the friend.

"You bet your life! I can't talk to my husband about it. He just gets angry at me—tells me to leave her alone—it's not worth the hassle. He says let her learn by experience. Do you think he's right?" asked the mother.

"I really don't know enough about it, Mary, but you do seem to feel that the problem has to be resolved soon, don't you?"

Note that the friend in this illustration twice avoided going beyond providing acceptance and getting involved with the "problem" itself. In the latter part of the example, the friend rejected the mother's request for an evaluation of the husband's suggestion. In the beginning of the illustration, the friend could have questioned the mother regarding what might be described as "smothering" or over-indulgent behavior. In both instances the listener reflected her friend's concern, but did not become actively involved in talking about the substance of the problem. The listener at some later point might quite appropriately become more active. Tools for more active involvement are described below.

Clarification

When you are listening it may be apparent to you that the speaker is confused, and you may choose to help him or her gain increased understanding. Several listening tools which are more active than acceptance are used to provide clarification. We will illustrate three of these: *restatement, paraphrasing,* and *perception checking.* Briefly, these are three ways of sharpening communication. Each enables the helper to assist a speaker to be more precise about what the speaker means to convey. All three are based on a principle of learning called self-discovery. Self-discovery is a principle you can apply frequently in your role as a helper. The essence of the self-discovery principle is that people are more likely to remember and act on what they discover for themselves than what someone else tells them. This appears to be true for at least two reasons. First, by definition the act of self-discovery requires commitment and participation, and tends to value most those things to which we commit ourselves. The second reason why self-discovery is effective, is that the individual is able to focus on what is seen as the important aspect of the problem. It's the perception of what is important that receives the attention. A teenager, for example, in a parental conflict is more likely to be motivated by discovering that certain behavior is causing others unhappiness than by the parents' complaint that he or she isn't shouldering responsibilities. The latter message passes through the brain without making an impact. It doesn't relate to his or her concerns. In contrast, discovering that one's behavior affects other people for whom one cares gets attention.

In spite of the importance of self-discovery, helpers often want to tell other persons where they are confused and to point out the errors in their thinking. You may become impatient with what you see as the folly of their ways and the confusion in their thinking. But that, of course, is part of their problem. Let them deal with it. To thrust your insights on them often only adds to their confusion. In addition to trying to clarify their own concerns, they now have to deal with your impatience and perhaps your erroneous observations and conclusions. There are times, of course, when it is helpful to confront individuals rather directly and forcefully with their inconsistencies of thinking and action. A parent who preaches thrift and spends foolishly, a friend who asks for psychological support and then rejects it because it highlights inadequacies, and patients who request prescriptions but fail to use them, may well benefit from being confronted with their self-defeating inconsistent behavior. We'll consider the skill of confrontation in another chapter.

Restatement The first clarification tool we will discuss is *restatement.* It's repeating to a person what he or she has just said, using his or her own words to the extent that seems reasonable. Restatement can contribute to increased understanding. People sometimes don't actually mean what they say. They may be hiding behind vague and general language. Hearing what they have said may result in their providing a revised and more precise statement to you. They are also, in the process, providing themselves with clearer thinking and thus increased self-understanding. Parents and teachers often use restatement with children.

In the following example a child, angry after an argument with his brother, shouted at his mother:

"I hate Bobby, all he ever does is try to get me in trouble!"

"You hate Bobby, all he ever does is try to get you in trouble," restated the mother.

"Well, not always," the child corrected, "but whenever we have a fight he won't stop when it's over. He always does something afterwards."

"He always does something afterwards," she restated.

"Yeah. You know—he tells on me, or takes something from me. You know. He does one more thing—I guess he thinks he wins that way."

In the illustration the mother used restatement to help her child increase his own understanding of a concern. She may or may not have understood the concern herself. Had she understood she could have offered an explanation, but that probably would have been rejected because it would have ignored the child's anger. Restatement acknowledged both his concern about unfair treatment by his brother and his anger regarding it. The question of whether or not he is right at this point is not the issue. Contrast the foregoing illustration of restatement with a different kind of response:

> "I hate Bobby! All he does is try to get me in trouble," shouted the child.
> "You don't really mean you hate your brother," corrected the mother. "He does some nice things for you."
> "I do too hate him! He's mean! The only reason he does nice things is to get in good with you and Dad."
> "He's not mean, and that's not fair," the mother responded defensively.

In the first example, the use of restatement acknowledged that the child had a concern which seemed legitimate to him. It also provided the child feedback of what he had said, thus giving him an opportunity to express his concern more accurately. In the second example, the mother began by rejecting both the boy's feelings and the legitimacy of his problem. Rather than focusing on the child's concern and attempting to help him clarify it, she placed him in the position of having to defend himself.

People often convey something other than what they mean for the listener to understand. Restatement provides the speaker with an opportunity to correct the inaccurate impression of the listener.

In the following illustration an office manager is discussing a possible promotion with a member of her clerical staff:

> "So, your references are very good," the manager declared. "The only thing you need to do in order to get the promotion is pass the next level secretarial exam."
> "That's what bothered me. It would be impossible for me to pass the exam. I don't have the ability," claimed the secretary.
> "You lack the ability," restated the manager.
> "No—I don't mean I'm not smart enough," she corrected herself. "I mean I would have to increase my shorthand speed and learn to operate the calculator."
> "I see," the manager replied.
> "It's not so much ability," she continued, "but whether or not I can find the time to get ready for the exam."

The two problems stated by the secretary are significantly different. If the problem is lack of aptitude, there is little the supervisor can do to help.

If, on the other hand, the problem is a matter of finding preparation time, there are several things the supervisor can do to be helpful, such as rearranging the secretarial work schedule and assignments.

Paraphrasing Paraphrasing is restating in your own words what another person's words convey to you. Paraphrasing does not involve a value judgment on the part of the listener. It does, however, involve one's making a judgment regarding what seems to be important to the speaker. Paraphrasing is used to clarify communication in several ways. Sometimes you paraphrase as a means of indicating that you understand what the other person has said. You also paraphrase when the substance of the other person's statements appears confused. In this case, paraphrasing is like a wager. You, as the listener, bet that you can make a clearer statement of the speaker's concern than the speaker did. The risk, of course, is that you may not. Even so, your response may still be helpful because the speaker, realizing that something is not clear, will try again. Obviously, if you attempt a series of paraphrases, none of which seem to the speaker to help very much, that person may conclude that you are not very bright.

Paraphrasing is a function of the helper's perceptiveness. "Listen" for perceptive comments in the following.

Mr. Smith, a teacher, is conferring with a parent of an elementary school child regarding the child's inability to follow classroom routine. The teacher summarizes what he has just explained:

> "So, Bobby does not stay at tasks as long as the other children, won't stay in his seat during study periods, talks at inappropriate times and often distracts other students."
>
> "That's about as clearly as I can expain it, Mrs. Williams. I thought maybe you could help me understand Bobby. How do you think he's reacting to school this year?"
>
> "He's always been active, you know," the mother stated. "Even as a little fellow—before going to school—he gave me fits. We always had to watch him like a hawk in order to get him to do things he was supposed to do. During the day it wasn't so bad—his jumping from one thing to another didn't bother me so much—but in the evening when Bobby's father was home—he can't stand confusion—then I just seemed to need to follow Bobby around to see that he did everything he was supposed to do."
>
> "Then Bobby has always been one to drop one activity and begin others— but you and your husband differ somewhat on the seriousness of this," said Mr. Smith, paraphrasing the mother's statement.
>
> "Yes—at that time I thought it was not good to constantly nag at Bobby—but it seemed necessary to keep peace in the family, at least in the evenings. During the daytime I suppose I didn't nag as much."
>
> "So perhaps Bobby got two messages about following through—one during the day and another at night," suggested Mr. Smith.

"I never thought of it that way, but I suppose it's true," Mrs. Williams agreed.

In this illustration the teacher was paraphrasing the mother's general description, attempting eventually to set a frame of reference for comparing Bobby's behavior at home with that at school as a means of developing a plan for helping him. Mr. Smith decided that it would be helpful to distill the mother's description to the essence of what she seemed to be saying, namely that reactions to the child's short attention span had been inconsistent at home.

Paraphrasing is also a function of skill with words; look for paraphrasing as a volunteer in a crisis clinic talks with a teenage boy:

"Would it help to try and explain the situation to me?" asked the counselor.

"I don't know—it's so damn confused," the boy replied. "My old man has all these silly rules see—well not silly—I mean when I think about them later they're not, but most of the time he comes up with these statements—what do you call them—announcements—and I just want to scream. I don't know the word to describe it—how I feel—but it's my life and he won't even listen to me—just makes statements without even letting me say where I'm at. Do you understand?" he asked.

"You don't resent the rules so much as you resent your old man not allowing you to help make them," the counselor paraphrased. "It's his making pronouncements that gets to you."

"Yeah, that's about it. But what the hell!"

"Well, it may be an important difference," she suggested.

"How do you mean?"

"The problem of avoiding having rules altogether is different from the problem of how to get your father to let you help make them," she explained.

"Okay, I see the difference, but so what?"

"It's this," said the counselor. "I can't help much with the first problem. But maybe I can help you with the second,"

In this example, the helper was able to use a word (resent) which was in the teenager's listening vocabulary (that is, he understood its meaning) but not in his normal speaking vocabulary. Most of us have a larger listening than speaking vocabulary. Part of the skill of paraphrasing is to bridge the gap between the two.

Perception checking Perception checking is a tool similar to paraphrasing but focuses on the feelings involved in the communications. Perception checking is a means of determining whether or not your assessment of another person's emotions or feelings are accurate. As we talk with another person we observe both verbal and nonverbal behavior from which we infer the feelings the person is experiencing and expressing. The individual may, for example, swear, talk hurriedly, wring the hands, or avoid eye contact. It is natural to make inferences regarding the feelings behind this behavior. It is important to remember, however, that the same kinds of behavior may indicate different feelings for different people. That being true, it is important that you check the correctness of your inferences or perceptions before acting upon them in order to (1) measure the accuracy of your perceptions, and (2) convey a message to others that you are aware of and concerned with their feelings.

Imagine you are a supervisor. The time has come to have the annual evaluation interviews with your staff. Many of them take this in stride, but some become nervous and upset and arrive for their interview keyed up with tensions. Recognizing this with a statement such as, "You seem nervous today, Dan. I imagine it's about the evalution" or "This is in some ways a trying experience, isn't it, Delores?" communicates your perceptions to Dan and Delores and gives them an opportunity to confirm or correct your observations. Delores might confirm your perception, and thus give you an opportunity to help reduce her tension so that a more productive interview can be held. On the other hand, Dan may tell you that he's not upset about the interview. Rather, he indicates that he is preoccupied and upset about a minor auto accident he had on the way to work this morning, and whether or not his insurance will cover it. In this instance, you might want to postpone the interview until Dan was in a better frame of mind for concentrating on the evaluation. Admittedly, perception checking appears like an obvious thing to do. But think of the number of times people don't examine the accuracy of their perceptions. Misunderstandings often result from people making incorrect inferences about other people's feelings. Harry speaks sharply to Bill, who infers that Harry is angry. In fact, Harry is not angry, but has an upset stomach. Barbara's perplexed look is taken as a sign of displeasure by Sandy, but is actually an expression of confusion. Simple perception checking by Bill and Sandy could have clarified communication.

When you are checking perceptions, it is important to avoid implying criticism or evaluation. *How* you check perceptions is often as important as *what* you check. Voice inflection or tone, the choice of words, word emphasis, and facial expression can easily convey criticism or evaluation. Indeed, it is impossible to be totally nonevaluative. The fact that you respond to another's feelings conveys some evaluation that they are significant. The point is to minimize criticism and evaluation by being sensitive to how you do perception checking. For example, the phrase "I have the feeling you are upset" is more effective than "You sure seem out of sorts," and "I seem to be confusing you" is better than "You still don't understand, do you?"

"This conversation is difficult, isn't it?" is preferable to "You're getting uptight, aren't you?" In other words, focus on your perception without being threatening. Describe your perception of the other person's feelings. Take responsibility for your own perception and ask the other person to check its accuracy. Don't assign feelings to the other person.

Probing

Probing is a way to ask purposeful questions. Active listening often involves putting questions to the person you are attempting to help. Sometimes the questions are asked so that you can gain a better understanding of the situation. They are also used as a means of helping an individual clarify something for himself.

There is nothing especially technical about probing; we all frequently ask questions in the course of a conversation. There is one aspect of probing, however, that can make your questions more helpful. It is the awareness that the degree of specificity with which a question is stated can affect the thinking of the other person as he or she provides an answer.

Consider the following example. Becky, a friend of yours, is talking to you about the possibility of changing jobs. After describing both the current and new jobs, she concludes:

> "So its really got me confused. The new job pays better, and I think has new opportunities—but I'm not sure I know enough about it. And moving would be expensive—and might harm the kids. It's occurred to me, too, that maybe I'm more interested in getting away from the unpleasant relationships at work than in the new job itself, and that might be a mistake."

Becky is obviously confused. You decide that a little probing might help her sort out her concern. There are three general levels of probing you may use. You can make an open-ended probe, or a probe directed at a particular concern, or one aimed at a specific issue. The following three questions illustrate these three levels. Reread Becky's statement. Think about your purpose in assisting Becky clarify her concerns, and then select one of the following probes:

> "It is complicated, Becky. What do you think about it?" [an open-ended probe]

> "It is complicated, Becky. What seems to be the chief source of conflict?" [a directed probe]

> "It is complicated, Becky. What is it you would like to know about the new job?" [a specific probe]

The questions represent three levels of specificity and are likely to produce different kinds of answers. In the first or open-ended probe, you are assuming nothing about specific issues or concerns. If you asked the first question you probably thought to yourself:

> "Becky is confused and I'm not sure she's got it all out yet. Let's get her to talk some more, but let's try not to influence what she'll talk about. If she keeps talking, she'll probably begin to reveal her chief concerns."

The first question, in other words, is very open-ended. When you ask, "What do you think about *it?*" you let the speaker define *it*. The second question or directed probe is less open-ended than the first. If you asked the second question you had probably decided that Becky had mentioned most of the issues involved. You decided that it would now be helpful for her to assign priorities to them.

If you asked the third question, you had either decided that one issue was more important than the other, or perhaps that each issue ought to be examined by itself and selected one with which to begin. In a specific probe it is the listener, not the speaker, who suggests the topic.

Many people who "listen for a living," such as counselors and lawyers, use open-ended probes at the start of a helping relationship, becoming more specific as the person they are helping reveals a clearer understanding of his or her concern. This would appear to be common sense. You are more likely to use common sense in probing if you remember that the degree of open-endedness of a question influences the scope of the speaker's thinking.

There is one further comment regarding probing which may be helpful. We have all heard a question which is actually a statement of the speaker's point of view. Is the probe an attempt to help a person clarify, or is it actually your veiled conclusion or advice? For example, when you ask, "Do you think that your attitude toward your son might be somewhat unfair?" or "Are you sure you've looked at it from your wife's point of view?" are you responding to something which seems unclear to the speaker in an attempt to help him gain understanding, or are you really offering your own "diagnosis"? If it is the latter, and the other person rejects your answer, you are likely to change his focus from understanding himself to dealing with the threat you may pose to him. This can be a subtle occurrence, and before you realize it, you may change from the role of helper to that of defender of an idea. When you find yourself primarily interested in getting the person you are attempting to help to accept your ideas, it is likely that you have lost much of your objectivity about the situation.

Through practice you can become skillful at using these three active listening communication tools: acceptance, clarification, and probing. We urge you to use them the next time you have an opportunity to be an active listener. You may feel clumsy or awkward at first, but with a little practice you should find that you are using the tools comfortably and naturally. Their use can become second nature to you.

CONTENT AND FEELINGS

So far in this chapter we have discussed and illustrated several basic communication tools. We have also made a distinction between the content of what a person is saying and how he feels about that content. At this point we want to expand and offer more detailed information about that distinction.

Statements can have many meanings. For example, someone says to you, "You must have paid a great deal for your new coat." He could mean:

1 I admire your coat.

2 I admire your good taste.

3 You look nice.

4 You are a spendthrift.

5 It looks terrible on you.

6 I envy you.

7 I resent your having more money than I.

8 You're trying to put me down, or

9 More than one of the above.

In other words, the statement may or may not have anything to do with the cost of your coat. If it doesn't, and if the speaker is really expressing his resentment of your good fortune but you take him literally, then some confusing interaction may follow.

The distinction between content and feelings is especially important in helping situations because people being helped frequently have significantly strong feelings regarding their concerns. If they didn't, the concerns wouldn't be important.

One can miss the whole point of a communication by not watching for both content and feeling. While not intending to play down the content of statements made by people desiring help, often the most immediate response one can make is to the feelings they are expressing. This is particularly applicable in the cases of vague complaints. There is little one can do in response to vague complaints except acknowledge the unhappiness, frustration, anger, or whatever feelings are being expressed. What can you say, in regard to content, in response to statements such as:

"The system is unfair."

"She doesn't understand me."

"How am I supposed to put up with such inefficiency?"

"I should have been given the promotion."

One can make inferences about what the speaker means and wants, but those would be largely speculation. There is a simpler way in which you are more apt to be correct in acknowledging the feeling being expressed. For example, in regard to the first complaint, you would probably be more effective to acknowledge that "You seem upset" than to guess why the system is unfair. And, the most productive response to "She doesn't understand me" is probably something to the effect of "You're disappointed."

An effective helper is able to recognize and respond to feelings as well as content. When Gloria says to her teacher, for example, "I'm really upset over this unit in algebra—I just don't get it, and I'm worrying so much I can't concentrate on any of my other courses!" she's expressing two concerns. A teacher who responds with, "Well, let's see if we can pinpoint what it is that you don't understand" is responding only to content. The student is also expressing some strong feelings. There is nothing necessarily inappropriate with responding to content, but frequently a helper can be more effective if he at least acknowledges the expressed feelings. Perhaps, as in this example, the teacher might be more helpful with the algebra concern if he acknowledged and even encouraged Gloria to describe her feelings before dealing with the content problems. If she did, a dialogue something like this might have occurred:

"I'm really upset over this unit in algebra—I just don't get it," said Gloria. "And I'm worrying so much, I can't concentrate on any of my other courses."
"Your worrying over algebra is affecting the rest of your classes," reflected the teacher.
"It sure is! I can't concentrate on anything. Every time I begin to study for another class, I start worrying about algebra."
"Why do you think it is so important to you?" asked the teacher.
"I was afraid of it from the first. I knew I couldn't do math!"
"You actually began to worry before you started the course?" the teacher suggested.
"I guess so."

"Well, let's look at it this way. You've come to me with the problem, so now we can get to work solving it. As we make some progress, you'll probably feel better."

"I hope so."

"Let's see if we can find out what's wrong."

This could be helpful in two ways. First, by sharing her feelings, Gloria may reduce some of her tension and anxiety, and thus put herself in a better feeling state for working on the substance problem. Second, by attending to feelings, the teacher is demonstrating concern about Gloria as a person, not just as a math student. Knowing that the teacher is generally concerned may increase the probability of her benefiting from help with the algebra.

There are some situations in which the helper is not in a position to be directly helpful regarding content. About all you can do is respond to the feeling. The following example illustrates this kind of situation.

The father of a teenage boy had been conferring with his attorney regarding some property contracts. As the conference came to a close, the conversation went something like this:

"Well, that seems to do it," said the father. "Christ, I wish we could resolve the 'pot problem' as easily as we took care of these contracts. My kid has me running scared all of the time. The damn laws about pot are ridiculous. I never know when he's going to get busted—and for something that's really not all that serious."

"It can really get you up tight, can't it?" noted the attorney, accepting the client's feelings.

"It sure does, and I feel like my hands are tied. I can't follow the kid around all the time, and it's primarily the legal thing I'm upset about. Hell, they catch him with a can of beer and it's nothing. They catch him with pot and he can really get hit."

"It does seem unfair. Many of my clients who have teenagers are frustrated over the same thing. It's an unpleasant aspect of being a parent these days," he acknowledged.

"You said it! It's easy to forget you're not alone in this damn thing," agreed the father.

By reflecting the father's feelings, not focusing on the law, and reminding him that others were facing a similar concern, the attorney may have helped the father change to a less anxious feeling state. Note that he didn't moralize or attempt to explain or justify the law. Such responses might have provided the father with new information, but would the information have been helpful?

The distinction between content and feelings is not always an easy one to perceive. Many of us become conditioned to focusing on content and become insensitive to expression of feelings. This is understandable. Very often the function of helping is to respond to people's requests for information and certainly this is appropriate. While responding to both feelings and content is often helpful, we are not suggesting that it is always appropriate. Sometimes dealing with the content is of paramount importance. In such instances feelings, while they may exist, are irrelevant to solving the particular problem. When a patient calls his dentist and says he is about to leave on a trip and he just lost a filling, it would not be especially helpful for the dentist to respond with, "You must feel very frustrated."

When we respond to the apparent content of such statements, it may seem to the other person that we are not communicating very well. Nevertheless, people very frequently make statements in content terms, that are primarily expressions of their feelings. Consider the following, in which Margaret, a junior high school girl, was talking to her mother about a situation at school:

"The class is really stupid," said Margaret. "Mr. Smith talks on and on and on, and boy, is he conceited. He always has to tell us how it was when he was in school. I wish I could get out of his class!"

"Have you talked to your counselor? Maybe you could change to another class," her mother suggested.

"Yeah. You know," Margaret continued, "he said that when he was in school kids had more respect for teachers. He says kids had to earn the right to express their opinions. How can you begin if you don't get some practice?"

"There may be other ways to practice—you know at home with us and with your friends," replied her mother.

"Oh, Mother, that's not the same! Boy if he knew what it's like to sit there and listen to him day after day. Somebody ought to let him know just how much he turns kids off. Somebody ought to tell him!"

"Could some of you go to your counselor and talk to him about it? Maybe he could help you talk to Mr. Smith."

"Oh, Mother!"

In this illustration, the mother missed the intent of her daughter's remarks. She was not offering poor suggestions; they are perfectly reasonable. But Margaret didn't want answers to her questions. She was simply expressing frustration over Mr. Smith's class. Her intent was to share her feelings with her mother. The mother's role as a helper, had she responded to the feelings the girl was expressing, could have been to provide acceptance, and if appropriate help Margaret clarify her feelings. Let's look at one way the mother might have focused on Margaret's feelings:

"The class is really stupid," said Margaret. "Mr. Smith talks on and on and on and boy is he conceited. He always has to tell us how it was when he was in school. I wish I could get out of his class!"

"It's pretty frustrating," reflected her mother.

"You can say that again. It's a real put down to have to sit there and take all of that garbage. I mean, he doesn't realize that times have changed."

"You wish that he could be more realistic about your generation," her mother suggested.

"Yeah. Well, maybe not realistic—I think he knows times have changed. I just wish that he would admit it—and that also he may have been more of a student than most of us."

"If he would clear the air, then what he does in class might be more acceptable," suggested her mother.

"I think so. You know, he's a very bright guy, and very interesting some of the time. It's just that he talks down to us so much."

"That's irritating," acknowledged her mother, "but it's a price worth paying if the class itself is worthwhile."

"I suppose that's right. Hey, guess what the big news is about the new drama coach!"

Following is an illustration of a helper attempting to respond to the feelings being expressed rather than to the content of the dialogue.

Two neighbors, Bill and Jim, are working in their yards and pause to talk:

"Damn!" Jim exclaims. "I resent having to keep up this whole yard by myself. I tell that kid of mine over and over to remember that he has to spend Saturday mornings doing yard work, but he's always got some excuse to get out of it."

"It can make you angry," Bill reflects.

"Damn right it can. He gets an allowance, uses the car, and everything else—all I ask is that he save one morning a week. In return for what he gets it's not too much to ask. He doesn't do a damn thing. I wish I knew how to get him to shape up, Bill."

"You feel like you are being had a little," replies Bill.

Bill could have suggested a means for getting the son to shape up, for example, making use of the car contingent on doing the yard work. But at this point, the suggestion would probably have fallen flat. Jim's main concern at this point were his own feelings, not his son's lack of cooperation.

Jim continues:

"I sure do. I guess it's really not the work that counts," said Jim. "It's more his not caring—not contributing to the family—that makes me angry."

"You'd like it better if he'd take a little responsibility," suggested Bill. "You might even like each other better—be more pleasant all the way around."

"Man, I think so!"

"Have you ever told him that—how you feel, I mean?" asked Bill.

"Sure, I tell him all the time to get some work done. It's one big hassle—that's the problem!"

"No," Bill clarified. "I mean have you ever told him how you feel about it? The feeling you have towards him when he doesn't help out? You said that was the important thing."

"Now that you mention it, no. I just get mad. Hey, maybe I'll try that. It might work. Nothing else has."

In the illustration, Bill, the helper, went beyond simply reflecting Jim's feeling. But even so, note that he didn't offer a solution to the problem as stated by Jim. He was perceptive enough to see that it was Jim's feelings about his son that had not been dealt with, and gently suggested that Jim deal directly with them by letting his son in on the real source of his anger.

The distinction between content and feelings in verbal interactions is not always easy to discern. We can easily misinterpret both. But we urge you to be sensitive to both in helping situations.

THE TROUBLE WITH WORDS

The trouble with words is that they aren't perfect. They are supposed to be firm symbols for things and ideas, symbols about which we all agree. But often they don't quite measure up. Words are imprecise, they don't mean the same for everyone.

"How far is it to town," asked a stranger to the area.

"Only a short way," answered the long-distance runner.

"Oh, a very long way," replied the small child.

"Divorce! My God, I can't even contemplate the possibility," exclaimed the wife of 18 months.

"Divorce? The standard fee is about $600," announced the seasoned lawyer.

The meaning of words depends upon your experiences, situations, and concerns. Problems develop when people forget that simple truth. Language is probably the single most important consideration in helping situations. It is both the essence of problems and the tool for solving them. Misuses of language can lead to all kinds of negative conditions such as anger, fear, disappointment, confusion, jealousy, and resentment. And the careful use of language can make them go away.

Wendell Johnson, a psychologist and student of language, suggested that half of the solution to a great many problems was being able to clearly describe them. Think about that. "I'm confused; I can't put into words what bothers me" or words to that effect is how many people relate a problem. "If I could just tell you what I mean, I would know what to do"; "I wish I could express myself better"; "I'm about to explode but I can't describe how I feel"; "It's a small kind of irritation, you know, but I don't quite have the words to describe it."

And when problems are resolved, we often say something to the effect of, "Wow! I finally got it out" or "Now that I can describe my concern, the issue is so much clearer." There is so much to say about language and helping that one could write several books on the subject (Johnson did).[1] Within our space limitations, we can only suggest how knowing more about language can be helpful. Specifically, we will conclude this chapter by (1) pointing out the importance of remembering that language is symbolic, (2) suggesting the difference between the world of words and nonwords, (3) noting that never is everything said about anything, (4) exposing pronouns, and (5) recalling that some of us don't talk and listen as well as others.

Language and Symbols

It is important to remember that language is symbolic; that is, words have no meaning in themselves. Language has meaning only when we assign some symbolic importance to it. Words come to mean something only when we give them meaning. Usually the assignment of meaning is purposeful and mutually agreed upon. For example, when we all agree to call that four-legged object which we sit on while eating dinner a "chair," then the word "chair" has meaning. When we also agree to call that overstuffed thing we sit on after dinner a "chair," then the meaning of the word "chair" has been increased.

This kind of common agreement about the meaning of words is what makes verbal communication possible. While a one-word, one-meaning language might have some advantages, ours is clearly more complex. We often agree that some words can mean more than one thing. Take the word *mean* itself, for example. In addition to the sense in which we have been using "mean" (to define, denote, signify or symbolize), it also stands for several other things. These include cruelty (as in, "That's a mean thing to do to him"); midpoint (as in the mean or average score); method (as in, get there by whatever means you can); and so forth. Now all of these meanings of "mean" usually don't cause us much trouble because as we learn the language we also learn to pay attention to the context in which words are used. So, when someone comments that "you play a mean game" of tennis, you smile and say thanks. You know from the context that they don't intend to

[1] Wendell Johnson: *People in Quandaries,* Harper & Row, New York, 1946.

say that you play a cruel game or even an average game. Someone just learning the language, however, and who was still at the one-word, one-meaning level, might think he was hearing nonsense. Another reason why a one-word, several meanings language isn't totally confusing is that new meanings are normally added over a long period of time. Language develops slowly and usually plenty of time is allowed for us to learn and get used to the new meaning assigned to words.

Words may mean different things to different groups. Consider, for example, a grandmother who was offended and thought poorly of her teenage granddaughter when the latter announced at a family dinner that, "I finally have my shit together." Her siblings didn't blink an eye, but grandmother gulped, nearly dropped her fork, and became visibly red in the face. Why? Because the word "shit" symbolized vulgarity for the grandmother—to the granddaughter it "stood for" the concerns, responsibilities and tasks with which she was presently confronted. She meant only to communicate that she had herself organized. She had no intention of using a vulgar word (or more precisely, a word which symbolized vulgarity). As a matter of fact, she thought she was conveying something about which her grandmother would be pleased.

What actually happened, however, was family discord due to the use of a word. The grandmother was upset by the symbol the granddaughter used, and not her behavior. The girl might think to herself, "What have I done to upset grandmother?" Obviously, the problem was not what she did, but how she described it. If you were to help change the negative feeling in this situation, you would focus on the language aspect of the situation. Similarly, when a teenage offspring, or a frustrated employee, or a confused student tells you to "Fuck off!" you will probably react quite differently than if they had said, "Please don't bother me right now. I'm too upset to respond rationally to what you want to say to me." Why? Both statements mean the same; just the symbols used to convey the meaning are different. It is fairly common in this kind of situation for people to generalize their negative reactions about a word to include the user of the word.

A related source of difficulty with words as symbols is that some people alter the meanings of words without consulting the rest of us. When they do, it can be upsetting. We usually refer to these as "problems of semantics." It is the "Oh, we don't mean the same thing" problem.

Virginia tells her husband that she got "drunk" at a women's club luncheon and he becomes angry and sulks for several days. "Drunk" to Virginia means feeling good after a martini, but to her husband "drunk" signifies stumbling incoherency.

Bill, a salesman, tells the sales manager that he nearly "blew the company image" with a prime client. Bill means to say that he was guilty of a small social offense with a company client, but carefully rectified the situation. His sales manager takes him "literally" and makes a mental note that Bill ought to be watched carefully.

In each of these examples, the difficulty stems from the symbolic meaning people assigned to words, and not the words themselves. Language works to the extent that it has the same meaning for all of those who use it. While it is true that most of us can tolerate a band of meanings, it is often wise to define the width of the band.

Clarifying meanings of words can often be very helpful. When language symbolism is part of a problem, helping people clarify definitions may be sufficient assistance.

World of Words and World of Nonwords

Those things for which words stand (the world of nonwords) are dynamic, in contrast to language itself, which is relatively static. For example, your name will remain the same once it is given to you, but you will change. You as a thinking, feeling, behaving individual are different each day in subtle ways. Over a year or decade, you may change significantly. Your values, interests, and abilities may have changed so much that today you are quite a different person than you were ten years ago. But the symbol we use for you (your first name) doesn't reflect any of the changes.

Now this may seem to be an insignificant matter but it can be important. For example, in 1968 Sara and Bill were married. Recently, their relationship has become very dissatisfying and disturbing. Both have been attempting to resolve their problems by trying to reestablish their original relationship. In a sense, of course, this is a futile effort doomed to frustration, essentially because Sara–1968 and Bill–1968 are not Sara–today and Bill–today. Each of them has made significant changes, and their circumstances are very different. Yet the language they use to talk about themselves and their relationship doesn't readily call their attention to the fact that they are now different people with different desires and interests who can only develop a *new* relationship based on Sara–today and Bill–today. They are trying to solve a current problem with out-of-date facts and information. Their language refers to the outdated circumstances of 1968 and obscures those pertinent today.

Probably the most important thing to remember about the relationship of the world of words to the world of nonwords is that it is imperfect. Seldom are we able to describe exactly how we feel or what we saw or heard. Few people have the ability to communicate exclusively with verbal language. Try, for example, to tell someone how to tie shoe laces without demonstrating or using your hands. And more to the point, try to fully describe your concerns and feelings about an important issue to someone. Or, try to completely understand the concerns and feelings of someone else. While there is great merit in continually trying to perfect the relationship between the worlds of words and nonwords, an immediate practical solution is to assume that you will be misunderstood some of the time and that you will sometimes misunderstand others. If we accept misunderstanding as a natural part of using language, then we are less likely to become upset when it occurs. Similarly, one can often be helpful in conflict situations by reminding people that confusion and semantic difficulties are to be expected and can be resolved.

Always More to be Said

Another notion that can be helpful is that seldom has everything been said about a subject. Information which appears complete and accurate today may not be tomorrow. Consequently, we should not be surprised when we discover that we do not have all of the information which we want. When circumstances regarding an issue change, people are likely to change some of their feelings and thus there may be something more to say. The importance of this observation can be seen in situations where after having reached an agreement with another person, the other person shifts positions on us:

> "I thought we had an understanding," states the frustrated father to his son. "You said you would come home immediately after school and do an hour of homework."
> "I did say that," replied the son, "but I didn't know about this special meeting after school."

The point is not to sympathize with the father or berate junior, but simply to illustrate that there apparently was more to be said on the subject than either had believed. Language can seem so final, so complete. When we have said something, it is easy to forget that even though our talk has stopped, the thing we are talking about goes on.

"What time is it?" As soon as you answer that question, you are wrong. New events and changing circumstances partially invalidate much of what we say at a given moment. In fact, most everything we say of any significance includes the "understood" phrase "assuming everything remains as it is now." But, of course, it won't, and thus there will be a little more which can be said about the matter. Whether or not to say it is another issue, but remembering that the world goes on when language stops can help avoid a good deal of confusion and unhappiness.

Pronoun Problems

Language problems are caused by the sloppy use of pronouns and collective nouns. Pronouns are convenient devices in that they give us some options for avoiding boring repetition. Without pronouns, we would have to say, "Bill went to Bill's office, phoned Bill's home, and asked Bill's wife to get Bill's wallet out of the coat Bill wore yesterday." Pronouns are fine as long as they have referents and we know what they are. Pronouns without clear referents, which don't stand for anything, can cause all kinds of problems and their continued use makes helping very difficult.

Among the chief villains are, "they," "it," "those guys," "the company," "the government," and similar words. These words seem often to refer to mysterious people and forces that are impossible to find but have great effects on our lives. When people attribute their problems to such mysterious sources, the most effective kind of help is often to assist them to clarify their pronouns and referents. What do they stand for, if anything? When this is resolved, the problem is usually stated more precisely and is more open to solution.

Consider George and Fay, who are trying to decide on a seating arrangement for a large company meeting:

> "The most important thing," suggests Fay, "is to seat the people who will be doing most of the talking at the head table."
> "Well, I don't know," George replies. "You have a point, but they may be upset if they're not up front."
> "Who are 'they,' George?"
> "You know, 'those guys' in the front office. They'll be upset if the spotlight isn't on them. We better have 'em up front."
> "Which guys, George?"
> "From the head office, of course," replies George, beginning to lose patience with his naïve coworker.
> "Let's be specific, George. Which of the people in the head office will be upset if they aren't at the head table? Especially if we tell them why. I would guess out of the ten or eleven, only Smedely."
> "Yeah, you're probably right," George agrees.
> "Well, then, let's see what we can work out for him," Fay suggests.

The obvious conflict in this little drama is a pronoun which George hadn't bothered to define. When Fay came to the rescue and helped define "they" as only Smedely, the problem was not nearly as difficult as George had assumed.

Individual Differences

People differ greatly in their ability to use language. This notion is particularly important because language is often used as a tool to compete for "things" including attention, money, time, and love. Those with lesser language skills are at a disadvantage in such competition.

When people with minimal language skills are confronted with a clever-tongued opponent, they may be in trouble. Rather than proceeding carefully, they may resort to shouting, name-calling, or withdrawing from the situation. Usually the shouting, name-calling, and withdrawing are ineffective. In any event, they are of little value in making one's point. No one really wins because attention to the initial concern is diverted to the new task of self-defense.

As a third party you can often be a referee seeing that people with weak language skills have their say. This isn't to suggest taking sides, and it may at times be appropriate to say as much. Sometimes a straightforward comment such as, "It is difficult for Eldon to get his point across. Let's be sure he has enough time." When time isn't the issue, then paraphrasing or summarizing can help: "It seems to me that Eldon is saying . . ." Even the use of probing can help some people better state what they are not communicating by helping them focus more clearly on their concern.

Two Questions

A final idea in regard to the use of language in helping, is to call attention to two short questions: "What do you mean?" and "How do you know?" If these were the only two language tools you had and you used them judiciously, you would undoubtedly be helpful to many people.

Katie meets her friend Lynda after work and seems to be feeling low:

"Anything the matter, Katie?" Lynda asks.

Katie answers and sighs, "I'm really not making it on my new job. I'm about to fail."

"What do you mean?" asks Lynda.

"Oh, everything is wrong. I'm just not catching on, at all."

"Everything? Be specific, what do you mean?"

"Well," answers Katie somewhat impatiently. "I made mistakes in writing up two orders and I didn't complete my daily report correctly."

"Did you do anything right?" Lynda asked with a smile on her lips.

"Sure. Everything else went okay, but I make a couple of important mistakes every day. And that is bad."

"How do you know?" Lynda continues.

"What do you mean, how do I know? I just know!"

"Does someone tell you? Are you corrected?"

"No," Katie replies. "I just feel bad when I screw up. In fact, everyone is

very nice to me. Miss Roberts even said I was selling more than most beginners
. . ."

Many, many problems are magnified and even created because someone is not being clear about a concern. People overgeneralize, operate within impossible vagueness and as a result conclude that the world is going to
hell in a hand basket. So the first question is often "What do you mean?"

Even when we clarify that, there is still the possibility that our observations and facts may be wrong. Thus, the second question is "How do you
know?" A very clear description of concerns can be developed from a completely erroneous observation. You must have observed or participated in
arguments which began to diffuse as soon as someone acknowledged that,
"Well, I assumed . . ." or "But at the time it seemed to me that . . ."
People do all kinds of unfortunate things to each other for clear-cut concerns based on totally inaccurate observations and assumptions. Try the
two questions on yourself. The next time you become upset or concerned,
tell yourself what is wrong. Then answer the question, "What do you
mean?" In all probability you will give a more accurate and specific description of your concern. Then, answer the "How do you know?" question.
Is your concern based on fact? Assumption? What someone told you?
Fear? Wishful thinking? Guilt?

Try the questions the next time they seem appropriate in a helping
situation. Remember, don't try to answer them for another person. Don't
even elaborate. Just ask them and be still. See what happens.

SUMMARY

This chapter described three active listening tools: acceptance, clarification,
and probing. The distinction between content and feeling in communication was described and several ideas regarding language were noted. The
underlying concept of this chapter has been the importance of communication in both the cause and solution of human problems.

EXERCISES

1 Now that you have read about communication, let's spend a week practicing the communication tools. Do the following for the upcoming
week:

Monday   Use restatement in two situations.

Tuesday   Use paraphrasing twice.

Wednesday   Use perception checking twice.

Thursday   Use perception checking twice.

Friday   Use the three levels of probing.

Saturday   Use probing twice.

Sunday   Summarize results.

Use the form that follows to collect data. First note the skill you intend to use. Then at the end of each day, briefly describe the situation in which you used it and the results you observed. What did you learn about the tool? About its use? Is it one which you can use effectively? What other tool could you have used?

DAY	SKILL USED	SITUATION	RESULTS OF USING SKILL
MONDAY		1. 2.	1. 2.
TUESDAY		1. 2.	1. 2.
WEDNESDAY		1. 2.	1. 2.
THURSDAY		1. 2.	1. 2.
FRIDAY		1. 2.	1. 2.
SATURDAY		1. 2.	1. 2.
SUNDAY: SUMMARY			

After reviewing each day's efforts, what general statements can you make about the effect these skills have on the quality of communication?

Which skills do you need to practice more?

When and where could you practice these skills?

2 Do you know the ways you show interest in other people? List five. Be specific (e.g., "I use expressive hand gestures," "I maintain eye contact"). During the next day or two use these ways you communicate interest and observe how other people react. In column 2 describe the effect each type of interest usually has on other people.

WAYS I COMMUNICATE INTEREST	EFFECT OF BEHAVIOR
1	1
2	2
3	3
4	4
5	5

3 List five ways you demonstrate acceptance of other people. Again, be specific (e.g., nod head, touch people). Describe how people respond to each kind of acceptance.

WAYS I CONVEY ACCEPTANCE	EFFECT OF BEHAVIOR
1	1
2	2
3	3
4	4
5	5

Did you have difficulty with communicating interest or conveying acceptance? Both can be difficult. It may be useful to continue practicing at least one behavior that shows interest and/or acceptance for one week.

Five | Goal-gaining Tools

WHY GOAL-GAINING TOOLS?

The previous chapter described active listening tools, those communication skills which are the basic tools of helping. The outcome of using these tools is to enable you and the person you help change feeling states and develop a clearer understanding of issues and problems. Sometimes helping is limited to these two outcomes. These two outcomes may not immediately influence or change behavior. There are other times, however, when you can provide additional assistance that contributes to behavior change. Such situations generally involve an individual's (1) making a decision or reaching a goal, or (2) taking action regarding a decision or goal, or both.

The extended help calls for additional tools. We call them "goal-gaining" tools. They are: *contracting, modeling, role playing, reinforcement,* and *decision making.* We stress goal-gaining tools because, as stated previously, a person with a problem usually wishes to change things as they are to things as they might otherwise be. When you are able to help someone translate wishes into specific statements of goals, you can use active listening to help them identify what they feel they *can* change, develop new confidence in what they actually *might* be able to change, and express fears about what they believe can never be changed.

Once you have helped clarify feelings and fears, you as a helper can then use goal-gaining tools to help someone think about making moves toward goals.

When a person states a goal, he is saying, "I would like something to be different." examples of goal statements are:

I want to make a decision on whether to stay married.

I want to pursue further educational training.

I want to know if I am well suited to be a working mother.

I want to spend my leisure time pursuing varied interests.

I want to make better use of my study time.

I want to acquire skills in parent-child relationships.

I want to get along better with my coworkers.

To reach a goal, that is to move to a point where "Things are more like I want them to be," requires new behavior. Sometimes what is required is imaginative thinking and planning. A new perspective, changed attitude, or insightful idea may be needed. In other situations a complex set of behaviors may be required. Skills for planning, coping with conflict, and dealing with occupational tasks may be involved. From the helper's point of view, goal-gaining tools are useful in assisting people develop new skills and new kinds of behavior.

CONTRACTING

A basic goal-gaining tool is *contracting*. A contract is an agreement between you and the person you are helping. The other person agrees to practice a certain desired behavior and you agree to provide assistance. The contract may be stated verbally or actually written. A contract makes clear who owns the problem and emphasizes that in order to use the helper's time and energy, the owner of the problem must take some constructive action. The following examples illustrate several uses of contracting as a helping tool.

Mary and Betty are neighbors. Betty is trying unsuccessfully to lose weight; she voices her frustration to Mary. Betty has a diet prescribed by her physician, but has not followed it. Mary suggests that Betty keep a written record of everything she eats for one week and that the two of them meet each morning to review it. Betty agrees, knowing that the meeting will be pleasant when she can report adhering to the diet and embarrassing when she hasn't.

Mrs. Black, a high school counselor, has been working with Gary, a sixteen-year-old junior, who wants to get a part-time job. She has helped Gary learn some job interviewing skills and to complete application blanks. Nevertheless, Gary is apprehensive and reluctant to actually contact employers. In order to help Gary, Mrs. Black uses contracting. After discussing the problem, Gary agrees to file applications with three employers. As part of the contract Mrs. Black agrees to review Gary's visits with him and help with the next steps. The contract helps assure that Gary will perform what was, for him, a difficult behavior. If he is successful, Mrs. Black can help Gary use his experience to begin building self-confidence.

John and Harold are friends. John reveals to Harold that he has been trying to tell his boss for weeks what he thinks is wrong with the project he is working on, but hasn't because it is his boss's pet idea. John says that he hopes to get up enough courage to talk with his boss tomorrow. Harold acknowledges that it is a threatening task, and asks John whether it would be helpful if they met tomorrow evening so that John could report his experience. John thinks that it would be helpful, and says that this commitment to report to Harold will motivate him to talk with his boss. Harold, without saying so, used contracting to assist John. The contract moved the helping situation from "It would be a good idea to talk with the boss," to a commitment to do so.

In each of these examples one person agrees to do something specific and then to report their behavior to another person. Generally, the steps in contracting are the following:

1   A goal is defined.

2   A plan is discussed, and the actual tasks to be done are defined.

3   The person responsible for doing the tasks makes a commitment to follow through.

4   The action is taken (or not taken).

5   A report is made to the helper regarding the action.

Contracting places the responsibility for taking the desired action on the person being helped. As a helper, you provide support, encouragement, and assistance in defining specific behavioral patterns, but it is clear that the person seeking help must act.

This also clarifies the role of the helper. Once a contract is made, the helper need not intervene until a report is made. When the report is made, the helper can offer support, may confront the individual with his failure to perform, or may renegotiate the contract depending, of course, on what is reported.

Because the terms of a contract are stated simply and directly, both parties involved can easily determine whether or not the contract was met. The action to be completed is clear to both persons involved. Think of the three examples just given. If the friend reports her calorie intake daily, if the student makes three job applications, and if John does talk to his boss, the contracts are fulfilled. There is no room for pussyfooting. Either the desired behavioral pattern has occurred, or it has not.

At first reading this may seem harsh. But let's look again. In the example of the neighbor who was unsuccessfully trying to lose weight, the friend could have listened for months about her good intentions *and* her failure to lose weight. Instead, the helper suggested a plan by which she could actually help her friend.

Mrs. Black, the high school counselor, could have talked and talked with Gary about why he wouldn't make a job application. However, once Gary had committed himself to wanting to apply, she provided the previously absent motivation. And Harold, who motivated John to actually express his concern to his boss, could instead have continued to listen to John gripe about the situation. In each case, the helper focused on a difficult task. Simply listening to the other person's concerns might have been easier, but in the end not as helpful as contracting for action.

An important consideration in each example is that the person receiving the help had in fact made a decision. Had that not been the case, that is, if those wanting help were really undecided about what they wanted to do, the use of contracting would have been less appropriate.

Here are examples of dialogues which result in contracts.

Janet and Carol have been friends for years and have often confided in each other:

> "It's so discouraging lately between Dick and me," Janet said with a sigh. "It seems every time we talk to each other about something important, we end up hassling."
>
> "What do you mean?" asked Carol.
>
> "Well, last night, for example. First, we were talking about Judy's going away to college. By the time we were finished talking, I had told him he didn't understand his daughter, and he said I was pampering her. It seems every conversation ends up like that—we're saying something negative about each other."
>
> "Is is really like that all the time?" asked Carol.
>
> "I'm afraid it really is—either we're just making small talk or we're arguing. I mean it's neutral or negative but never positive anymore. That's awful to say, but it's true!" sighed Janet.
>
> "The problem is how to change things," suggested Carol.
>
> "It sure is," agreed Janet. "I care about Dick, but it seems like I just emphasize the negative things now."
>
> "Do you think making a conscious effort to change would help? Maybe you need to be pretty obvious at first. Do you ever tell Dick that he looks nice or that you appreciated him doing something you asked, or tell him that something he said is interesting?"
>
> "I'm afraid not—I used to."
>
> "Do you want to try it for a few days? Maybe you could say at least three pleasant things a day to him," Carol suggested.

"That sounds like a good idea. It's getting so that I'm feeling like a nag. But doesn't that seem a little stilted?" asked Janet.

"Probably at first. But why not try it? Maybe it will get to be a habit. Why not start tonight and tell me how it goes tomorrow?"

"Okay, I don't expect miracles," Janet said smiling, "but maybe it's a start."

In this example, Carol, as a helper, acquired a basic understanding of the problem and then asked Janet if she was interested in changing. She then suggested a desired behavioral pattern. This is fairly common in contracting. The helper proposes the behavioral pattern based on their mutual understanding of the problem. Sometimes the contracted behavioral pattern needs to be discussed and clarified. This was not the case with Janet. She knew what it meant to say "pleasant things," but she had not done it for some time.

The last task in contracting is to listen and respond to the individual's report. The next example of contracting illustrates the "reporting-back" phase.

Reverend Widmark had been talking with one of his church members, Mrs. Rice. Mrs. Rice, a healthy and formerly vivacious person, had been telling Reverend Widmark she felt depressed recently. After the last of her children had left for college, she felt more and more depressed. At first her husband had been supportive, but now he was becoming resentful of her complaining about how meaningless life had become. Mrs. Rice indicated that she wanted to become active again. On a number of occasions she had decided to take some action which would put some meaning back into her life, but she just couldn't seem to get started. Reverend Widmark decided to use contracting as a way of helping her. At the end of the talk Mrs. Rice had committed herself to phone a garden club to inquire about membership, and to visit an art center to find out what classes would be starting within the month. Reverend Widmark agreed to see her in a week and hear a report about how things had gone. She returned after a week and the following conversation took place:

"Well, how did it go, Mrs. Rice? What did you find out?" asked the Reverend.

"I don't know what to say—I just didn't feel like contacting those places—I meant to do it," she replied.

"What do you think went wrong?" he asked.

"Oh, I don't know—I don't seem to care that much. Well, I do care but I just couldn't make the effort."

"Does it still make sense to get involved in the kind of activities we talked about last week?"

"Yes, if I could just get up the gumption to do it," she agreed.

"I understand this is a difficult period for you, but I'm going to be fairly firm. If I'm to help you, you must follow through on your decisions. Shall we try it again?" he asked.

"Well, I know I have to move—I guess anything would be better than this! I'll try to carry through this week on what we agreed to last time," she promised.

"Fine. When will you contact the art center?" he inquired.

"Well, I guess I could see them on the way home."

"Good. Now to help you keep your commitment, will you call me about five o'clock this afternoon and tell me what happened?"

"Okay."

Contracting, then, is a tool useful for motivating people to take action once they have reached decisions or established goals. You may be a little uncomfortable the first few times you use contracting. That is a natural reaction. When confronted with situations similar to those in the previous examples, many of us typically just sit and listen or attempt to give advice. If that is typical of your response to such situations, contracting will be a new behavioral pattern for you. But, it's not a difficult tool to learn if you will practice it. Remember, a good contract is made after a decision or goal is established, and it includes a clear statement of what is to be done, and usually how often.

MODELING AND ROLE PLAYING

Modeling and role playing are useful helping tools which are often used together. *Modeling* is demonstrating a behavior to another person. *Role playing* involves practicing or experiencing a behavior in a nonthreatening situation. Obviously, role playing often follows modeling. Through role playing people practice the behavior they have observed being modeled. Nevertheless, we will discuss each somewhat separately because role playing has other uses besides practicing modeled behavior.

Modeling

Much of our behavior is learned by attempting to imitate other people's actions. The people we imitate serve as models for us. Modeling is common in daily life. Review a few of the things you have learned via modeling. As a child, your parents probably served as a model for much of your learning. By observing models you learned to tie your shoes, brush your teeth, eat, dress, answer the phone, adjust the TV, and a myriad of skills you now take for granted. School also involved modeling. You observed the physical education instructor demonstrate the correct technique to use for shooting baskets and then you tried it. You listened to foreign-language recordings and then you attempted to pronounce the words.

Television is a powerful modeling source for young children, affecting a full range of social behaviors and even thinking processes. Children learn values regarding marriage, money, occupations, sex, and every other part of their culture via the modeling of TV. There are literally thousands of behavioral patterns that we learn by observing models.

Thus, modeling is not new to any of us. But what might be different is the conscious use of modeling as a helping tool with personal problems. Modeling is often viewed as an acceptable means of learning skills such as swimming, dancing, knitting, and languages but often rejected as a means of learning more personal skills such as making decisions, talking effectively with a child, negotiating with a spouse or expressing feelings. Nevertheless, modeling is an effective means of learning personal and social behavioral patterns.

When used purposefully as a means of learning new behavior, modeling involves both observing and practicing. As a helper your intent is to create a nonthreatening situation in which other persons can observe someone practice the behavior and then try it themselves without embarrassment. Persons may appear inept as they begin to practice a new behavioral pattern, but they will not feel as uncomfortable as they would if the new pattern was attempted in a real setting. The following example illustrates this point.

June, a housewife, wanted to talk with her husband about the negative manner in which he often responded to their children. She was anxious about doing so because she couldn't think of an easy way to start the conversation. During a talk with a friend, she mentioned her concern. The friend offered to model two ways in which June might resolve the problem. First, she demonstrated a means of getting the husband's attention before he became defensive. She suggested that June say something like the following:

> "John, something is bothering me, and I want to talk to you about it. I'm nervous because you will probably find the subject unpleasant. But I still want to talk with you and get your opinion. I want to say my piece carefully, so will you give me five minutes before reacting? Just five, and then I'll listen to you."

The friend demonstrated, not just talked about, the statement. She then asked June to practice similar statements using her own words.

The second solution she modeled was to write a brief note to her own husband asking for a chance to calmly discuss a problem. She had June read the note, then tore it up; June then wrote her own note, and the two women reviewed June's note together.

A primary advantage of modeling is its potential for building self-confidence. In the example, June not only became aware of two ways to deal with her concerns, but she also practiced them. She demonstrated to herself that she could do what she had learned. Just talking about what she might do would probably have been less effective than modeling and practicing.

There are many kinds of modeling procedures. We will limit our concern to two of these: (1) demonstrating the desired behavior yourself and (2) using someone other than yourself as a model. In deciding which helping procedure to use, that is, whether you or another person should do the modeling, ask yourself two questions. First, can you, as a helper, perform the skills or behavior in question? Second, even if you can, will your modeling be seen as realistic and believable to the person you are trying to help?

In the previous example, June's friend believed that she could model the desired behavioral pattern herself and that she had enough credibility with June to be seen as realistic. When credibility is an issue, one can often find more appropriate models. For example, Harry, a high school counselor, included several sessions on interviewing for jobs in his program for graduating seniors. In past years he had modeled interviewee behavioral patterns himself, but was not satisfied with the results. Students had commented "Sure, you can do it, Mr. Green, but that's different. You have some advantages." Consequently, Harry asked two students who had graduated the past year and had obtained good jobs to assist him. They modeled correct interview behavior. Because students could identify with the recent graduates, they were more effective models than Mr. Green. Similarly, counselors who work in rehabilitation settings have used rehabilitated clients as models because they have more credibility than the nonhandicapped counselors.

Modeling can be done in real settings, as the following illustrates. Ethel, a girl in her late teens, had been seriously overweight most of her life. She had shown no interest in clothes or participating in social situations. She had recently become determined to improve herself and get more out of life. She had been successfully following a weight reduction program and now wanted to purchase more attractive clothes, but she was almost totally inept at selecting attractive wearing apparel. She revealed her problem to a girlfriend who was skillful at selecting attractive attire. The friend volunteered to go shopping a couple of times with Ethel. On these trips she identified clothes which were suitable for Ethel as well as some which weren't, stating the reasons in each case. She then suggested that Ethel choose some clothes and state why she selected them. The friend, in other words, modeled clothes selection behavior for Ethel.

How, as well as what, you model is important. Show some enthusiasm. Think realistically about the person you are helping and the situation in which the new behavioral pattern will be used. If possible, get a decision on how much the person wants to practice. It is also important that you avoid being self-conscious, for if you are, the person being helped is likely to be self-conscious also. When the behavioral pattern is practiced, respond first to the things done correctly. If the first performance is absolutely inappropriate or not productive, then respond positively to willingness to at least try the behavioral pattern. In other words, structure the modeling situation in such a way that total failure is almost impossible. This is an important point. We once used modeling to help a young college woman learn social skills. The woman was painfully shy and quiet. Initially we modeled doing "small talk" in a two-person, two-minute casual situation. This didn't work, so the goal was reduced to modeling responses to greetings offered by co-workers such as, "Good morning, Sally. What's up for today?" Even this seemed too much for the woman. About all one could respond to positively was her willingness to try. We began modeling again, but this time concentrating on specific behavioral patterns such as making five-second eye contact, smiling, then combining eye contact with smiling, responding to salutations with short sentences such as, "Hi, I'm fine. Looks like a good day." Eventually, the woman was able to learn a set of social skills via modeling.

Obviously, this example represents an extreme situation, but many new behavioral patterns must begin at a very elementary level. The point in presenting this example is to illustrate the importance of (1) you as a helper being realistic about what can be learned by an individual and (2) structuring the modeling situation so that you can respond positively to the person's performance. When a young child is learning to tie shoes, the child ought to be rewarded initially for getting a string in each hand, not chided for failure to make a knot.

Role Playing

Role playing is a procedure similar to part of the modeling procedure just described. That is, when individuals practice a new behavioral pattern, they are in effect playing a role—namely their own. As a helper you may sometimes decide that modeling a new behavioral pattern is unnecessary in a particular situation. It may be enough to simply suggest that you will play the role of a third person (e.g., spouse, child, supervisor) while the person you are helping tries out some new behavior on you. The person gives a self-portrayal, attempting to practice the new behavioral pattern. In such instances, you, as a helper, decide to short cut the use of modeling and go directly to role playing. In essence, you believe that the person you are helping can perform the desired behavior if simply given an opportunity to practice it in a safe situation.

For example, Marge, a woman in her forties, decided she wanted to go to work. She thought that some occupation in publishing might suit her, and she made appointments to interview two editors. She was nervous about the interviews and mentioned this to a friend. The friend suggested they role play an interview. Once they were into the interview, the friend added to its value and interest by asking questions such as, "Don't you think you're a little old for this game?" "Will your husband allow you to work?" and "Can you deal with men?" Some humorous answers and exchanges resulted. Thus the friend provided a good learning experience, and also by the use of humor, helped reduce Marge's apprehension regarding the actual interviews. They couldn't be any more difficult than her friend's role playing.

There are other uses of role playing. One is using role playing to help another person gain a more accurate perception of the feelings and values of someone with whom they are in some sort of conflict. Another is to help another person experience being in a particular situation or living with a certain set of characteristics similar to those of a person with whom they must interact.

A role-playing situation where one takes the role of someone with whom one is trying to communicate allows a person to understand better how that person sees and experiences the situation. For example, when a mother and daughter are arguing about whether or not an 11 P.M. curfew is fair, they might change roles, each trying to act as if she were the other. Or a supervisor, attempting to explain to an employee why a particular policy is important, might ask the employee to assume the role of supervisor to (1) deal with an imaginary employee who won't adhere to the policy and (2) experience the supervisory perspective. In these role-playing situations it is likely that the mother and daughter, and employer and employee, will understand the other's perspective better after "walking in their shoes." In either case, they still might not agree with the other person, but the rapport and appreciation of the other's position should be greater.

The use of role playing to gain a better understanding of an individual with characteristics foreign to your experience involves simulated experience. For example, volunteers preparing for work in a medical center for paraplegics could spend a day in a wheel chair playing the role of patients. A custodian or secretary beginning work in a school for blind children could themselves be blindfolded for several hours, and assigned tasks similar to those which the children must perform daily, such as eating, dressing, finding the bathroom, and bathing. As a helper, you might ask an over-demanding parent to play the child while you play the parent and insist that they obtain permission for and report each action they take. Or a parent of an alienated teenager might be asked to play her child while you play the role of a concerned, confused, and uptight parent. This use of role playing enables people to gain an understanding of perspectives and circumstances which are unavailable to them in real life.

The principles underlying role playing are similar to those of modeling. First talking about techniques of interpersonal relationships is often not sufficient to make those techniques a part of one's behavior. Role playing helps translate theory into practice. Second, maximizing involvement and direct participation in learning new behavioral patterns makes it more likely that they will be learned. Role playing is not a spectator sport. It requires participation. Third, the more similar a role-playing situation is to the real situation, the more likely the behavioral patterns practiced will be used in real life.

As a helper you will probably find that many people resist role playing. They may protest that it is "silly," "artificial," or "just a game." One way to overcome such resistance is to acknowledge that role playing is much like a game, and then to point out that one can often learn by playing a game. And there is nothing terrible about feeling silly for a little while, especially if something can be learned from the experience. You can also explain the three principles just noted. It is usually important to review or "debrief" following a role-playing situation. Debriefing is a means of reviewing and learning from an experience and will be discussed in the next chapter.

REINFORCEMENT

In the final analysis, most of us do whatever we do because some reward is anticipated. Rewards can be external or internal. External rewards are those provided from a source outside oneself. Examples are candy, money, love, affection, praise, respect, popularity, special privileges, and job promotions. Throughout our lives we depend upon external rewards. But as we mature we learn to reward ourselves internally. Examples of internal rewards are feeling appreciated, satisfaction about a job well done, pleasure regarding living up to a principle or value, and feeling proud about not succumbing to a temptation.

The systematic use of rewards to help a person learn or perform a behavioral pattern is called *reinforcement*. In its basic form, reinforcement is simple enough. It consists of identifying a desired behavioral pattern and then rewarding the person each time the desired pattern is performed. You might want to reward a child for proper brushing of teeth, or a husband for saying something pleasant to his wife in the morning. A person might even want to give a self-reward for leaving the room when feeling angry with a child but knowing the situation is not right for resolving the problem. In the three examples just noted rewards could consist of a penny, a smile from one's wife, and the avoidance of an unpleasant experience with a loved one. When a behavioral pattern is reinforced it becomes stronger. That is, it is more likely to occur again. When an individual has decided upon a goal or a desired behavioral pattern, but can't seem to get started towards achieving it, reinforcement can be a useful helping tool.

Note that there is a difference between reinforcement and bribery. The sense in which we are using reinforcement entails the assumption that the individuals you are helping have made their own choice about "how they want things to be different." Even though they may find the new behavioral pattern difficult to do, they have declared that they want to do it. Bribery also makes use of reinforcement but with a very important difference. Bribery uses reinforcement to foster a behavioral pattern an individual does not want. To attempt to control others against their will is beyond the bounds of helping.

Certainly, an individual may not like to practice a particular behavioral pattern because it is difficult or inconvenient to perform, but may, at the same time, agree to perform it because in the long run the outcome is seen as desirable. A person who is overweight may not like running two miles each morning before breakfast, but at the same time agrees to do it because of the hope it will help him or her to lose twenty pounds. In this illustration losing twenty pounds is the goal, and each day's small decrease in weight as measured by the bathroom scales is the reinforcer. A teenager who wets the bed four or five nights a week may not like to set the alarm and arise at 2 A.M. for a trip to the bathroom, but is willing to put up with the inconvenience if it will result in dry sheets every morning. Waking up in a dry bed is the reinforcement for getting up in the middle of the night.

As a helper you can use reinforcement in two general ways. First, you can take responsibility for providing the reward yourself when a person performs as desired. Second, you can assist another person to establish a reinforcement plan which is independent of your involvement. Our main emphasis in this section will be on helping others establish their own reinforcement plans, as contrasted with your providing the reinforcement. We will discuss the latter briefly at the end of the section.

There are three principles of reinforcement which can guide your efforts:

1   The reinforcement should be consistent. Haphazard reinforcement, in which behavior is sometimes rewarded and sometimes not, is much less effective than providing a reward each time the desired behavioral pattern is performed. The goal is to associate practicing the pattern with a pleasant outsome. Inconsistent reinforcement is weak at best and can even confuse the person, thus creating an unpleasant situation which is not conducive to learning.

2   Reinforcement should follow as soon after the behavior as possible. Reduce to a minimum the events which take place between the behavior and the reward. Every minute or event which separates the behavior from the reward lessens the strength of the reward.

3   The reward and the behavior to be performed should be clearly defined and linked. The individual should clearly understand the relationship between the behavior and the reward. Many things which can be used as rewards are not natural outcomes of the behavior in question, and thus both need to be specified precisely. For example, if you decide to reinforce doing homework with use of the family car on Saturday night, you and your teenager should have a clear understanding of both the behavior (homework consists of an hour's study each weeknight between 6–9 P.M.) and the reward (using the car means he can take it at 6:30 P.M. and must return it by midnight). The reason for urging specificity is fairly obvious. Following a decision to attempt new behavior, there are often temptations to avoid it, or cheat a little. When the behavior and the reward are vague, cheating is much easier to do than when there is no question about what is to be done and what is to be received.

The following examples illustrate helping others to set up their own reinforcement plans.

Cheryl and Joy were close friends. Joy dropped out of high school and twelve years later was taking correspondence courses in order to obtain her diploma:

> "It's so difficult to get into a study routine," Joy reported. "I have plenty of time during the day when the kids are gone, but I just can't seem to get anything done."
>
> "I can imagine it is difficult," agreed Cheryl.
>
> "I just seem to make up excuses not to get to it—the studying is not that hard—I just get tired of it quickly."
>
> "How do you study?" asked Cheryl. "I mean. how do you try to use your time?"
>
> "That's what's discouraging—I set aside three hours each morning for studying. I do my housework in the afternoon, at least that's my plan—but it doesn't work. I usually waste my mornings," Joy answered.

"How about doing it a little bit differently?" suggested Cheryl. You could study for an hour and then do the dishes. Then study for another hour and then do more housework. Then study again and go out and do some gardening."

"Somehow I thought I would get more done if I spent a lot of time on it, but I haven't. I think I'll try that," agreed Joy.

In this illustration the self-directed reinforcement plan was built around the idea, "If you study for an hour, you reward yourself by getting to do a different activity." The schedule is self-directed in that Joy chose the activities and was responsible for carrying out the schedule. But it also violates the third principle in that the behavior and the reward are vague.

Joy tried her plan for a week and then told Cheryl that it didn't seem to work:

"It starts out fine each day," reported Joy, "but after the first hour of studying I seem to get involved in the other things and just don't get back to the school work."

"Do you have a specific plan for each day?" her friend asked.

"Well, sort of—I have a general idea."

"Why not jot down the activities you want to do in each time period."

"How do you mean?" asked Joy.

"First make a list of what you will do each hour," Cheryl explained. "For example, 9–10 read history; 10–11 make beds and do breakfast dishes and clean the kitchen; 11–12 read English; 12 eat lunch and work outside; and 1–2 write assignments."

"That might be better; I'll try it," Joy agreed.

This time the plan worked. The example also illustrates that the nature of rewards is a very individualistic matter. Many women would not choose housework as a rewarding activity. Some would.

In the following illustration a helper assists in developing a reinforcement plan in a child-parent relationship.

Bruce, a junior high student, had agreed to help his working mother by doing certain chores around the house. He had agreed that he had a responsibility for doing chores because his mother was employed full time. Bruce had agreed to set the table for dinner and clean the kitchen after dinner. For this he was to receive a weekly allowance. But a conflict arose between Bruce and his mother because his mother wanted the kitchen cleaned immediately after dinner, but Bruce thought anytime before 9 P.M. was okay. His mother began to nag, and there was usually a hassle at allowance time about whether or not he had done his chores on time. Apparently the reward was not close enough in time to the behavior.

A friend had two suggestions for improving the situation. First, the mother might make seven equal payments, one each night after the work had been done. This seemed needlessly inconvenient and an unnecessarily childish approach to take with a fourteen-year-old boy. The second suggestion made more sense and worked. It was to add another reinforcer, a "social reward." That is, verbally praise Bruce immediately following or even during the time he was cleaning the kitchen. The friend suggested that the mother think of several ways to provide the social reward, and begin using them the next time Bruce performed his task on time. Comments such as, "Thanks, it really helps to get the mess cleaned up early," "I appreciate your cleaning up at my convenience," and "Your doing this on time makes my evenings so much easier," were identified and used consistently.

Reinforcement can also be a useful tool for resolving marriage problems. Henry and Martha had a reasonably happy marriage. Martha, of recent months, however, seemed discouraged over life in general. Typically she had taken great pleasure in doing a variety of activities for her family such as sewing, preparing special meals, arranging for family surprises, and in other ways contributing to happiness of the people in her family. Henry noticed that as she became more discouraged the frequency of these activities decreased. He tried to talk with her about her discouragement but the only noticeable result was that she became even more discouraged.

He mentioned his concern to a friend at lunch, and wondered if he had come to take his wife for granted. The friend suggested that perhaps what Martha needed was a more obvious payoff for her efforts and less talk about her discouragement. As a result of the conversation Henry made an effort to be especially aware of anything that Martha did which resembled her former efforts to make life interesting for the family. Each time he made such an observation he would acknowledge to her the worth of her contributions.

In other words, Henry reinforced the desired behavior with an explicit reward (praise) which had meaning and importance to Martha. As a result, the frequency of the desired behavior increased, and Martha became a much less discouraged person. We don't mean to be sexist in using the preceding example. The roles can certainly be reversed. At some other period in their marriage, Martha could use reinforcement to help Henry overcome discouragement or provide psychological support.

The next example involves a relatively structured self-reinforcement plan. Shelly was a very attractive young secretary working in a large office. During high school she had been a flirt and gotten a lot of attention from male students. She obviously enjoyed her popularity, and it caused her few problems. On occasion boys would become a little too aggressive, but she could deal effectively with them. Some of her girl classmates were jealous, but she generally enjoyed a favorable reputation. She was seen as a flirt, but not cheap or an easy mark, and her peers knew it.

After working only a short time, however, she found that her flirting got a very different response from many adult males, a response which made her uncomfortable and unhappy with the image others were developing of her. Her inviting smile, swinging hips, and subtle body contact during conversations resulted in offensive remarks, clumsy fondles, lunch and dinner date offers made with ulterior motives and finally open propositions. She revealed her unhappiness to a friend, and indicated that if she couldn't change her image she might find a different job and make a new start. Shelly indicated that she certainly wasn't a prude and enjoyed attention, but neither did she like being seen as cheap.

The friend asked if Shelly was aware of why men were responding to her as they did. Shelly acknowledged that she was somewhat of a flirt but couldn't be more specific. The friend asked if it would be helpful to have her impressions. Shelly said it would. The friend mentioned several things including Shelly's sexually provocative clothing, her habit of touching men when she talked to them, her tendency to lean close to men when she spoke to them, and that she often gave encouraging or at least neutral verbal responses to suggestive remarks made to her.

Shelly agreed that all of these things were true. But they were such a natural part of her behavior that she was not conscious of doing them. She thought that from now on she would be more aware of them.

The friend suggested that if Shelly were serious about changing her image, she could consciously practice some new behavioral patterns. Shelly agreed and said she would try to (1) dress in a more conservative manner, (2) refrain from touching when talking, (3) make an effort to stand less close to men, and (4) express her displeasure regarding offensive suggestive remarks. But she wasn't very optimistic about being able to make the changes, especially the touching and closeness.

The friend suggested that it might be helpful for Shelly to keep a record of the number of times she practiced the second and third behavioral patterns. Shelly thought that was a little contrived but agreed that it might help her remember to do them.

Obviously, Shelly wasn't going to make a dramatic change overnight. But she was more likely to reach her goal when she identified specific desired behavioral patterns and a means of rewarding herself for performing them. Recording the behavioral patterns provided one kind of reward, and reminded Shelly that she was performing the desired behavior. This awareness was pleasing. Another reward was provided by the friend. The friend contracted to review the week's events and the checklist and, if appropriate, compliment Shelly for her efforts.

The friend's compliments were reinforcers. Providing reinforcement to another can be done in conjunction with contracting. When it is, it is advisable to structure the relationship between you and the person you are helping. Problems can arise when you use yourself as a source of reinforcement and you need to be careful regarding just what behavior you are reinforcing. We spoke earlier of fostering dependent relationships. Such a relationship can be established unintentionally when you provide reinforcement. If, for example, you are providing praise to a person who is attempting to lose weight, is it the weight-reduction behavior you are reinforcing, or are you reinforcing the person's dependence upon you? One way to avoid dependence is to encourage the individual to look increasingly less to you and more to himself or herself for the reward. You might, in this illustration, begin by having the person report the weight loss to you once a day for a week, then every other day for another week, then once a week and then not at all. During the process, encourage the individual to develop an internalized reward. Encourage self-praise for performing well. The person's own pleasure over losing weight will replace your praise and, hopefully, will be sufficient to maintain the weight-losing behavior.

One final thought about reinforcement. We reinforce people as a natural part of our every day life. Every time we react to another person, we are in fact reinforcing their behavior. The reinforcement can be positive or negative. When we show a keen interest in what other persons are saying, we are providing positive reinforcement to their talking behavior. When we listen to them, we are saying in essence, "You're interesting and what you are saying to me is worthwhile. It's okay to continue talking." When, in contrast, we are inattentive we reinforce negatively. When we turn away or tend to some other task while listening, we are communicating: "What you are saying isn't of sufficient interest to hold my attention." The other person can even generalize and interpret your lack of attention to what is said as a personal rejection. The point is that reinforcement is not something new to you. You reinforce a variety of behavior daily. What may be new is the idea that as a helper you can use reinforcement more purposefully than before. In order to do this we have suggested that it is necessary to identify the specific desired behavior as well as what will be used as a reward for its being performed.

DECISION-MAKING TOOLS

Chances are good that in the last day or two someone has said to you, "Gee, I can't decide what to do." What was your reaction? Nothing? Did you listen? Did you offer comments or suggestions? Did you make a value judgment? Did you advise about what should be done? Or did you state that you would rather not talk about the problem?

At one time or another all of these may be appropriate responses, depending upon the circumstances which prevail. There is, in other words, no single best way to help another person with a decision-making problem.

Much has been written about decision making. Some call it a science, others an art, but one thing is certain: many of the decisions we make have a tremendous impact on our lives. In this section we will describe one particular procedure for decision making and illustrate how you, as a helper, can use it to assist people with decision-making problems.

Decisions, Predictions, and Uncertainty

Decisions can be difficult, frustrating and even upsetting. Why? What accounts for decisions often being difficult tasks? One explanation is that decisions by definition entail predictions and predictions involve uncertainty. Even simple decisions involve implicit predictions. "If I decide to wear my blue outfit, I will make a better impression on my client than if I wear my brown dress." "If I spend the afternoon with my daughter, our relationship will be better than if I don't." "If I take the old road to the city, I'll enjoy the trip more than if I take the freeway."

There is no guarantee that any of these predictions will come to be. Your client may not like blue outfits, you and your daughter may have a horrible argument which leaves bad feelings for weeks, and you may encounter a long wait due to construction on the old road. Basically you know that these or similar uncertainties exist. They could happen, even though you may not be aware of the specific possibility at the time you decide.

When we make decisions which are relatively serious, we tend to be more aware of the uncertainty involved. Many people are uncomfortable with uncertainty and that's why decisions are psychologically difficult. A decision implies the prediction: "If I do A, then B will occur." For example, "If I marry Jane, I will be happier than if I don't marry Jane." "If I go to college, I will live a better life than if I don't go to college." "If I accept the position with Xerox, I will have more opportunity for advancement than if I accept the position with Home Town Enterprises."

If we knew what we wanted, and if we were certain that A would lead to B, then the decision of whether or not to do A would not be difficult. Often, however, we are not sure of what we want and uncertain that the action being considered will actually lead to it.

Jill and Doug, who have been married for twenty years, think that they want the freedom of being single, but are not totally sure. How much would each enjoy the freedom of living alone? How much would it be depressing?

Would starting new lives be exhilarating or mostly frustrating? Are there actually pleasures in their marriage which couldn't be possible without their current spouse? If so, is the trade-off worth it? They aren't sure. They may think that being single is what they want, but they aren't certain. And even if they were certain, they cannot be sure that getting divorced will lead to those things they associate with being single. The problem of child support, property settlements, relationships with relatives and friends, and financial loss associated with getting the divorce may result in their being less free than they are within the marriage. Their decision is difficult because they are not clear about what they want. "Being single" is still a fuzzy concept to them and they are uncertain that becoming divorced will make things as they want them to be. That's what we mean by prediction and uncertainty.

There are two kinds of information we can use in making decisions. The first is information regarding the predecision situation, and the second is our evaluation of possible outcomes of the decision. Prior to a decision, we have a goal which is more or less clear; we may also have factual information—the advice of others, our own experience, expert judgments, and wishful thinking. To some mix of these we add our feelings about the possible outcomes of the decision. How important is it to impress the client? Does the relationship with the daughter need some attention? What are the consequences of arriving in the city thirty minutes later than planned? What price are Jill and Doug willing to pay for being single? In other words, what are you risking if you decide to do *A?* The difficulty of a decision, then, is a function of:

1   The clarity of our goals

2   The quality of our predictive information (How certain are we that doing A will lead to B?)

3   The importance of the outcome

4   The risk involved (what we can lose)

For example, suppose you are trying to decide whether to spend the afternoon playing golf or going to a movie:

1   Clarity of your goals
    —You want to have a pleasant afternoon and don't especially care how.

2   Predictive information
    —The weather report calls for rain (70 percent chance).

—A movie reviewer with whom you usually agree gives the film a favorable rating.

3 The importance of the outcome
   —Not serious, although it's your only free afternoon this week.

4 The risk
   —About $3 to $4 either way.

Ha! An easy decision! The movie wins hands down.

Consider a more complicated decision. We are trying to decide whether or not to purchase a vacation cabin as a means of strengthening family relationships and getting the children out of the city on weekends because they are getting into trouble in the city.

1 Clarity of objectives
   —We know that we want to build strong family ties, help the children avoid serious trouble, and have some positive experiences, but cannot be much more specific.

2 Predictive information
   —We know four families who purchased vacation places; two appeared to enjoy theirs, the children in the third refused to go, and the parents in the fourth got a divorce.
   —The salesman says it's an ideal place.
   —The kids are already showing signs of undesirable behavior.

3 The importance of the outcome
   —The kids are running with a bad crowd and will probably get into serious trouble unless some new activity is initiated to change their associations, or so we think.

4 The risk
   —It's more than we can easily afford; we'll have to borrow $10,000 for a down payment and repairs on top of monthly payments; might get it back, but it would take time; property isn't moving well.

Obviously, a difficult decision for several reasons. Our objectives are not clear, the predictive information is weak, the outcome appears important, and a significant amount of money would be risked. There is, in other words, much uncertainty. If we make a decision under these conditions, it is less likely to be satisfactory than if we had clearer values and better information. When people don't know what they want or how much they are willing to pay for it, satisfaction is difficult to obtain.

Some of the uncertainty could be reduced. To begin, we could be a lot clearer about our goal. What is the nature of the trouble the children may encounter? What city experiences do we want to avoid? Can these actually be avoided in a vacation area? What do we mean by strong family ties? What are examples? What specific weakness in family relationships needs attention?

We have almost no predictive information, but some is obtainable. We could visit various areas, trying alternative places. We could discuss the decision with the children. What are their preferences, concerns, and expectations?

Similar thinking about the importance of outcomes and the risks involved could add further information, and thus reduce the uncertainty. However, it is important to remember that most decisions which are significant will also involve some uncertainty because, after all, they entail predictions.

A Decision-making Procedure: Nine Steps and a Worksheet

A number of methods or procedures for making decisions can be useful to a helper. We will describe one which is general enough to be applied in a variety of decision-making situations.

Think of the procedure as a structure for making decisions and the facts and values involved as the substance of decisions. It is assistance with the structure of decisions with which you can be helpful. As a helper you can teach others how to apply the structure to their decision making. You can assist them to fit the bits and pieces of their decisions into a systematic process.

The nine steps of the decision-making procedure are described below, followed by an illustration. Refer to the "Decision Worksheet" on page 92 as you read the nine steps. It helps clarify the procedure. Please remember that in the interest of describing the decision-making procedure, we have broken it into specific steps. Only computers make decisions by separating pieces of the program into bits. But the procedure is easier to understand and practice when parts are separated.

The importance of being clear about goals cannot be stressed too much. Unless you know what you want, it's impossible to know when you get it. It follows that trying to help people who are unclear about what they desire is frustrating, and often futile until goals are understood. Keep in mind too that goal clarification is not a one-shot operation. Because people and circumstances change, stating and clarifying goals is an ongoing requirement for most people. The goals you held ten years ago regarding income, recognition, and advancement were probably different from what they are today. They'll also be different ten years from now. Parents' aspirations for their children can change from dreams of fame and riches to simply hoping they finish school.

People can get themselves into a lot of unnecessary misery when they operate from positions of unclear, inaccurate, and outdated goals. There is probably no more welcome relief from self-imposed pressure than to finally acknowledge that you probably won't become president of the company, make a great sum of money, or be best at whatever interests you. People who don't adjust their goals as they gain experience can see themselves increasingly as nonsuccessful. (A very relative term—success for some is doing the minimum required, while for others it is nothing short of being the best.)

Read the description of the nine steps and the example that follows before practicing the procedure.

1 *State Your Goal.* On a separate sheet of paper, describe "how you would like things to be for a situation in which things are not as you want them to be." Be specific regarding people, circumstances, and other conditions. Take time to be as clear as you can. When you have a clear statement of your goal, record it in space 1 on the Decision Worksheet. Try to avoid confusing a goal with an alternative means of pursuing it. For example, "obtaining a college degree," "getting a job," and "securing a divorce" are not necessarily goals. Sometimes they are, but usually each represents only one means of achieving a basic goal. "Obtaining a college degree," for example, is usually one means of gaining status or preparing for a job or becoming better informed. There are alternative means of achieving each of these three goals. The same idea applies to the other two examples. "Getting a job" is one alternative for acquiring money or engaging in a worthwhile activity, and "securing a divorce" is only one means of resolving marital unhappiness. It is not unusual to confuse a goal with one alternative means of pursuing it. When we do, of course, we become preoccupied with that alternative and tend to ignore others, some of which may be much more suitable to our actual circumstances. If you have identified several goals or problems, select the one on which you want to work.

2 *Identify Alternatives.* In space 2 list every possible alternative means you can think of for achieving the goal. If you can't think of any, ask others for suggestions and seek out information whenever possible.

Regardless of how impractical or foolish some ideas may appear, list them anyway. Hold off on value judgments for the time being.

3 *Clean-up Alternatives.* Now review your list of alternatives. Combine those which appear to repeat ideas and eliminate any which are so much in conflict with your values that you can't accept them.

4 *Predict Needed Resources.* In space 3 note the resources needed to implement each alternative. In addition to money and skills, these may include personal resources such as persistence, courage, support from others, and self-confidence. This often requires obtaining information regarding some or all of the alternatives.

5 *Be Realistic.* Eliminate alternatives for which resources are clearly unavailable or too difficult to acquire.

6 *Identify Risks.* In space 4 note the risks and undesirable aspects entailed in each remaining alternative. Risks in this instance refer to what you might lose by pursuing each alternative, and include such things as self-esteem and relationships as well as material items.

7 *Evaluate Risks.* Now use space 5 to rate each remaining alternative according to your willingness to accept the risk or experience the undesirable aspects involved. Use the following scale:

1 = Risk acceptable
2 = Risk mostly acceptable, some reservations
3 = Risk mostly unacceptable, very uncomfortable with it
4 = Risk totally unacceptable
Rule out all alternatives rated 4.

8 *Select.* Now, if you want to make a decision with minimum risk select the alternative which has the most acceptable risk level and for which resources can be obtained. If two or more alternatives have similar ratings, go to step 9.

9 *Introduce Your Values.* If low risk is not your most important consideration, then do an "alternatives preference ranking." To do this, first record the basis or criteria of preference in space 6. (Preference criteria can range from "impact on others" to "it feels good.") Then use space 7 to rank the alternatives according to your preference and without regard to the level of risk involved. Your first preference will be ranked Number 1, your second Number 2, and so on. Now choose the alternative which has the highest preference ranking *and* an acceptable risk rating.

DECISION WORKSHEET

1. GOAL							

6. PREFERENCE CRITERIA

2. ALTER-NATIVES	3. RESOURCES NEEDED			4. RISKS AND UNDESIRABLE ASPECTS	5. RISK RATING	7. PREFER-ENCE RANKING
	SKILLS	MONEY	PERSONAL	OTHER		

Example: Ann

The decision-making procedures can be learned with a little practice. Before using the nine steps, it should be helpful to study the following illustration.

Ann is married and has three children. She married the same month she graduated from high school ten years ago. The first baby came ten months after that, and the third baby arrived before her fourth wedding anniversary. Bob, her husband, began his junior year in college shortly after they were married. The initial years were difficult financially, but they did survive by borrowing from their parents, obtaining loans, and by Bob's working part-time. He completed his B.A. in Business Administration seven years ago. Bob has worked for a large retail department store where he is currently an assistant manager. He is often preoccupied with job concerns. Their debts have been paid off, and three years ago they purchased a comfortable three-bedroom home.

Doesn't sound so bad, does it? Well, Ann's life has changed quite a bit in the last months. Their youngest child is now in school, and thus Ann spends a lot of each day alone. Her enthusiasm about decorating the house and gardening has dwindled. Her relationship with Bob has been deteriorating for two years and has become particularly strained in the last few months, to the point that they are discussing divorce. Their discussions have not led to productive solutions.

Ann realized that other than her attempts to discuss the marriage with her husband, she has done nothing to deal with her dissatisfaction. Now determined to obtain greater satisfaction, she began to analyze her situation as a basis for making decisions. In the following pages we have noted some of her thinking as she used the decision-making procedure and have reproduced her entries on her decision worksheet (pp. 96–97).

Step 1: State Your Goal Ann began by noting several goals such as getting a job and joining volunteer groups. Then she realized that these weren't goals, but instead alternative means for obtaining "something else." After considerable thought she listed the following goals:

> To improve the marriage relationship or to resolve it in some way that will diminish the unhappiness it caused

> To develop new sources of career satisfaction that will provide a sense of contribution and worth

After further thought, she assigned top priority to the first goal and entered it on the Decision Worksheet. The second goal, while important, would be put aside until she made some progress on the first.

Step 2: Identify Alternatives Ann began by listing alternative ways to reach her goal. The first list contained these items:

Go to a marriage counselor with Bob.

Go to our minister with Bob.

Talk to other married friends about how they relate to each other.

Try a trial separation.

File for a divorce.

After talking with a friend, Ann added these alternatives:

Jointly read and try the ideas and techniques described in such books as *Marriage Happiness* and *The Mirages of Marriage*.

Join a couples group sponsored by the YMCA.

Devise an approach on their own for establishing effective ways to relate.

Ann thought this list probably was not exhaustive, but it seemed to contain a fair number of alternatives to consider.

Step 3: Clean-Up Alternatives Ann then reviewed her list for the purpose of identifying redundancies and clearly unacceptable alternatives. She rejected the last alternative on the list because it represented essentially the procedure they had been following. She also rejected the alternative of a trial separation because this seemed to be little more than postponing dealing with the problem. She entered the remaining alternatives on her worksheet as shown.

Step 4: Predict Needed Resources The next step was to determine the kinds of resources that would be needed for each remaining alternative. This took much time and effort on her part, and she found that it was necessary to imagine living each of the alternatives before she could identify all the resources that would be needed. The most difficult resources to pinpoint were the personal/emotional strengths that would be required if each alternative became a reality. To do this, she imagined the kind of interactions and negotiations that might occur with each alternative. Then, based on past experience, she predicted how she might react in each situation. On that basis she predicted the emotional resources which would be needed. The list that she developed is shown on the decision worksheet.

Step 5: Be Realistic The next task was to eliminate alternatives for which there were inadequate resources or for which the resources were too difficult to obtain. After reviewing the list, Ann decided that there was

DECISION WORKSHEET

1. GOAL: To improve marriage relationship or resolve it in some way to diminish unhappiness it causes.

6. PREFERENCE CRITERIA

1. Quality of help
2. Non-involvement of other people

2. ALTER-NATIVES	3. RESOURCES NEEDED				4. RISKS AND UNDESIRABLE ASPECTS	5. RISK RATING	7. PREFER-ENCE RANKING
	SKILLS	MONEY	PERSONAL	OTHER			
Marriage Counselor	Ability to select competent counselor. Ability to describe why I think this would be an effective alternative to Bob.	$25 an hour.	Courage to overcome initial fear of talking to "outsider."	Bob's coopera-tion	Might make situation worse by opening areas previously unopened. Might argue over spending $25 an hour.	2	1
Minister	Ability to describe why I think this would be an effective alternative to Bob.	None	Courage to overcome being embarrassed to describe personal problems to minister.	Bob's coopera-tion	I know minister much better than Bob. Might make situation worse by opening areas previously unopened. Might strain current friendly relationship with minister. Minister might not have training in marriage counseling.	3	3

Alternative	Skills/Abilities	Cost	Personal Requirements	Cooperation	Risks		
Talk to Couple Friends	Ability to describe why I think this would be an effective alternative to Bob. Ability to describe to friends how and what we want to talk about.	None	Courage to overcome embarrassment of describing personal problems to friends.		Might endanger our current friendly relationships with couples. Might make our relationship worse by opening areas previously unopened. Might start disagreements between the other couples involved.	3	5
Divorce	Ability to describe to Bob why I think this would be an effective alternative. Ability to make new life style for self—social, work skills. Ability to be single parent.	Lawyer's fees. Funds for separate household for Bob. Child support and alimony.	Courage and skill to deal with loneliness. Reactions of friends and family.				
Read Books Use Techniques	Ability to describe why I think this would be an effective alternative to Bob. Ability to jointly discuss and implement ideas presented.	Minimal	Self-confidence to engage in intellectual discussion with Bob.	Bob's cooperation	Might make situation worse by opening areas previously unopened. Might cause arguments of "You're not using the idea/technique right."	2	2
Couples Group	Ability to describe why I think this would be an effective alternative to Bob. Ability to discuss concerns in group.	$30 for 6-week	Courage to describe personal problems to strangers.	Bob's cooperation	Might make situation worse by opening areas previously unopened. Might get unqualified or ineffective group leader.	3	4

really only one alternative—divorce—for which the resources were not available. Ann felt that at the present time she did not have the necessary occupational skills, financial resources, or self-confidence to start a new life style as a single parent. Thus, she eliminated this alternative.

Step 6: Identify Risks   In the next phase of the decision making Ann enumerated the risks and undesirable aspects entailed in each decision. Again she found that she had to mentally estimate what would be involved. The risks and undesirable aspects she identified are in column 4 on the decision worksheet.

Step 7: Evaluate Risks   Ann rated the risks for each of the remaining alternatives, using the 4-point scale:

1 = Risk acceptable

2 = Risk mainly acceptable, some reservations

3 = Risk mostly unacceptable, very uncomfortable with it

4 = Risk totally unacceptable

As shown on the chart, Ann had no 4 ratings.

Step 8: Select   Ann still had five alternatives for which she could probably obtain the resources and which had acceptable risks. If she had been seeking a low-risk decision, then at this point she would have rejected the three alternatives with 3-risk ratings, and decided between the first and fourth alternatives. However, because she was not primarily interested in a low risk, she was willing to consider all of the five remaining alternatives.

Step 9: Introduce Your Values   Therefore she ranked the five in terms of her preference. The criteria she used were: *(a)* quality of assistance, and *(b)* noninvolvement of friends and other people, other than Bob and herself. Her ranking is noted in space 6 on the decision worksheet. As shown, she ranked seeing a marriage counselor as the preferred alternative.

Helping With Decisions

Remember that what we have described is a model for making decisions. As such it is useful in explaining how rational decisions are made. But few decisions would ever follow the steps just as they are presented. For example, some goal clarifications may come toward the end of the process, thus looping the decision maker back to begin again. Some alternatives may not occur until the process has been completed and a tentative decision made. Sometimes a person needs help with only one or two aspects of decision making. Some people may change the order of some steps. All we suggest is that the process as described is helpful in assisting people learn what is involved in making rational decisions. Given the decision-making procedure, how can you use it to help people who are trying to make important decisions?

First, when they are without a method for proceeding, you can teach them the nine steps. When faced with an important decision, it is not uncommon for people to become overwhelmed. Their thinking becomes confused and discouraged; they become tense and irritable, which only increases the confusion. The decision-making procedure, while no panacea, can provide an often needed structure upon which one can do some complex thinking. By explaining the decision-making steps, and assisting one to use them, you can help bring order to what may seem initially to be a chaotic set of circumstances.

As you use the procedure or some modification of it, you should become more skillful at helping people sort out their concerns and make effective decisions. In many instances simply explaining the decision-making steps will be sufficient. You will have provided a useful procedure; no further help will be needed. Remember that we are not suggesting that one complete the nine steps and the form for all of life's decisions. This would be ridiculous. The procedure is simply intended as a tool for teaching a decision-making process.

You can also use the communication and other goal-gaining tools to assist people with decisions. The remainder of this chapter illustrates using the tools in several steps of the decision-making procedure.

Stating Goals   By using the basic communication tools discussed in Chapter 3 you can often assist an individual to develop a more precise statement of his concerns and goals. Decision-making problems are often stated in very gross terms. The problem may be much more specific than initially stated. For example, "I don't like my job and I've got to decide upon another" may really mean, "I don't get along well with one or two coworkers," or "I lack several key skills which causes me embarrassment."

"I can't decide whether or not to marry Ron," may really mean: "Do I want to risk giving up my own career?" or "How can I overcome my frequent spells of loneliness?"

Accepting both the individual and the importance of the decision can increase that person's willingness to work on it. The use of the clarification tools and probing can help the person reexamine the circumstances faced and the individual's perception of it. These tools can also help identify and examine the importance of the emotional or feeling aspects associated with a particular decision. You can also use contracting and reinforcing to assist an individual to work on a problem which is avoided because it is unpleasant.

Identifying Alternatives   In addition to using the basic communication tools to help the other person identify alternatives, it can be helpful to suggest one or two yourself. This is especially helpful when an individual is locked into a problem and can't see the trees for the forest. When you suggest possible alternatives, these may be rejected as unacceptable, but the person may still understand that they are possible. You can, in other words, help one to understand the concept of alternatives.

Predicting Resources   At least two kinds of assistance can be provided in regard to predicting needed resources. The most obvious is to help an individual obtain information. (We will discuss providing information and present lists of specific information sources for various kinds of problems later.) In educational decisions, for example, people usually need relatively straightforward information regarding costs. This can also be true with personal decisions. For example, a couple contemplating a divorce needs information regarding attorney fees and court costs. In the heat of battle they often overlook getting such information. There are other kinds of less tangible resources entailed in many decisions, such as help in coping with loneliness, and the helper can also assist the individual to identify some of these.

Many times people don't realize the demands that a particular decision will place on their personal resourcefulness until after the decision is made. Again, the helper can use the basic communication tools to assist a person to try to anticipate just what these demands might be, and whether or not he or she has the resources to meet them.

Identifying Risks   In some instances the person you are helping may prefer not to reveal certain risks and values to you. You can still be helpful, however, by encouraging the individual to give them self-consideration. Also, encourage the person to make lists even if he or she shows them to no one. Writing the values and risks often makes them more real and tangible. In complex decision-making situations, the lists become added assurance that important factors won't be overlooked.

Selecting   Selecting an alternative is the tough step. You can, however, use the basic communication tools to help clarify the alternatives and their implications. You can also reinforce the importance of making a decision. But, in our judgment, you should be careful not to reinforce the particular alternative selected. The distinction is often difficult to make. As a helper you are attempting to reinforce the individual's completing the decision-making process, not the particular decision made. It should be clear that it is the individual's decision. The person may reexamine the decision a number of times in the future. In the event that is done, you want to minimize the opportunity for the individual to shift the responsibility for choosing the particular alternative to you.

When an individual selects an alternative which has some risk associated with it, somewhat uneasy or uncertain feelings may be experienced. This is a perfectly natural reaction, and it may be helpful for you to restate that this is so. We are not suggesting that you give reassurance that "everything will be okay," because it may not. But the person has made a choice and the outcomes of that choice are to some extent uncertain. It may be helpful to give reassurance that a certain amount of apprehension is normal.

So far we have been concerned with helping people make decisions when specific problems are apparent. There is another kind of assistance which also can be appropriate; that is helping people become aware of decisions which they could make. Some would label it consciousness raising and others reality clarification. Whatever the terminology, we have all observed people in varying degrees of unhappiness or dissatisfaction who act as if their situations were unchangeable. That they are in a potential decision-making situation simply doesn't occur to them. It is not that they decide not to do something about their circumstances; they don't recognize even the possibility of a decision.

Ernie provides an example of being unaware of potential decisions. He is employed in a large city. His salary is exceptionally high relative to his education and experience. He hates living in cities, and thus commutes about ninety minutes each way from a small upstate community. After a year of devoting three hours each day to traveling to and from work, his temperament began to suffer. Margaret, a friend, gently confronted him with his increasingly negative moods:

"I know," he acknowledged. "It's the commuting—I dread each evening and the ride home. And then I dread the mornings."

"You could live in the city," she suggested.

"That would be worse. I simply refuse to live in a little box in a big building next to more big buildings. It's impossible!"

"Then you really do face a pretty basic decision, don't you? I mean if commuting is really as bad as you say."

"What do you mean, basic decision? I have no choice, as long as living in the city is out."

"Come on, Ernie—you don't have to keep your job. You can decide to do something else. Get out of the city completely."

"Are you kidding? Where else could I make what I make now? And, besides, I like the work."

"Right, Ernie. You make very good money and you like what you do. But that doesn't mean that there aren't other important considerations, like spending three hours a day on the train."

"No, that's just the price I pay."

"My only point is, do you have to pay it? You seem to assume that your present income is a given—that it can't be changed."

"I suppose I do. I mean, doesn't everyone want to maximize his income?"

"Most do probably, but it is possible to *decide* what you prefer, not just *assume* that what you are doing is what you most prefer to do."

"Give me an example of deciding. Like right now, I don't have an offer of another job."

"Okay. But you could decide upon the maximum amount of time you are willing to commute. You could decide what is a minimally acceptable income level. You could decide whether a compromise between living in the country and the city is acceptable. You could make decisions about several circumstances which seem to contribute to your unhappiness."

Ernie, as do many of us from time to time, may be helped by having what he takes for granted challenged—unhappy marriages, family relations, school situations, poor working conditions, physical environments, and inconvenient policies and procedures. Practically any dissatisfying situation is potentially a decision-making situation. It can be helpful to make people aware of this when for whatever reason they have come to assume existing circumstances are inevitable and unalterable.

SUMMARY

In this chapter we described several tools for helping people gain goals. We discussed why decisions are difficult and suggested various ways in which you can be helpful regarding the various aspects of decision making. Contracting, modeling and role playing, reinforcement, and decision making are best learned through practice.

EXERCISES

1 Note in the left-hand box that follows, three goals you've achieved and three you've failed to achieve. Then in the right-hand column briefly describe why you succeeded or failed with each goal.

Does there seem to be some pattern to your behavior when you don't achieve goals?

What can you learn about your patterns of behavior when you are successful? Talk to two people who have recently reached a goal they were trying to achieve. Ask them to describe the process they went through to achieve the goal. Note why you think each person succeeded.

SUCCESSFUL GOALS	REASONS FOR SUCCESS OR FAILURE
! 2 3 UNSUCCESSFUL GOALS 1 2 3	1 2 3 1 2 3

PERSON 1	PERSON 2

Do the two people have similar or dissimilar goal-setting styles?

Which person do you identify with most? Why?

2 Consider for a moment one of your friends who occasionally complains to you about a specific problem (e.g., being overweight, smoking, poor budgeting, etc.). Think how you might design a contract for them. Outline your thinking below. Then consider how you would proceed with suggesting a contract the next time they complain to you.

3 List below at least ten things about which you often receive compliments. These can be interpersonal or more tangible skills (e.g., "You certainly speak well in front of a group" to "You make the best omelet I've ever tasted.")

Now your list.

What I do well

1	6
2	7
3	8
4	9
5	10

Now imagine that one of your friends admired you so much that they wanted you to teach them one of these skills. Think how you would model for them your expertise in this area. Remember, be specific, break it down in small steps. Outline your modeling procedure below for one of the skills listed above.

4 Preview an upcoming situation about which you have some concern (e.g., telling a coworker that his report is not well written, telling your child he can't go to the weekend social events, etc.). Describe it below.

```
DESCRIPTION OF EVENT:
```

Now take a few minutes to imagine yourself in the situation. What will the circumstances be? How might you approach the subject? Actually practice aloud what you might say in the situation. Reflect on what you've said. How will others react to it? Because of this practice (role playing), how might you act differently when the real situation occurs? What benefits do you see in role playing an upcoming event?

5 Identify a decision you want to make now or in the near future. Use the decision-making procedure and worksheet on pages 92–93 to make the decision.

Tools for Observing and Describing

Six | **Behavior**

Human behavior can be very complicated and troublesome, but it usually makes sense. The challenge is trying to understand it, to turn chaos into sensibility. The keys to understanding troublesome behavior are *accurate observation* and *effective description*. A business meeting which has turned into a nonproductive argument, a party where guests seem cold and uncomfortable, or a class which can't get down to work are examples of groups which can benefit from behavior observation. If one has observed the dynamics of a situation, it often can be helpful to describe them to the participants.

There are several behavior observation and description tools which can be useful in clarifying problem situations. The tools aid you, the helper, in determining *what* to observe and *how* to describe. They are useful as a means of bringing important information that bears on problems and issues to the attention of those who are in the problem setting. This chapter considers conditions in which observations are made, three tools for observing behavior, and three tools for describing behavior.

OBSERVATION CONDITIONS

We have arbitrarily divided the world of behavior observation into three conditions, one of which some people would argue isn't observation at all! The three conditions are:

Direct observation—unstructured: you, the helper, observe people behaving naturally; you don't give them instructions on how to behave.

Direct observation—structured: you, the helper, suggest a role or behavior to be performed which you can observe.

Indirect observation: the person being helped writes or tells you about the behavior in question.

There are several important differences among the three observation conditions. One is the amount of control you, the helper, have over what you observe. In unstructured observations you record behavior as it occurs naturally. The people you are observing determine what takes place. If, for example, you are helping a group where communication is sometimes a problem, your goal, under unstructured conditions, would be to wait until a problem arises and then describe individual and group behavior. It may be a while before one does. Having no structure or guidelines, much of their behavior may have little relevance to the problem with which you are helping.

Under structured observation, in contrast, you suggest the kind of behavior that you want to observe. In the previous example, you could provide structure by having the group role play a problem-solving session or suggest that they actually talk to each other about their problems. In neither case do you have to wait for relevant behavior to happen. The implication of structured observation is that you, the observer, have a fairly good idea of what you want to observe.

In helping situations where structuring is possible, it may be to your advantage to structure in order to get the most out of observation time. There are many situations in which even though structuring would be advantageous it would also be disruptive.

Consider the following two examples which contrast unstructured with structured observation. John and his daughter both agree that they "just can't communicate," and ask if you can help them discover the reason.

"Do either of you have any notion of what the problem might be?" you say.

"No," they reply, and agree that there just seems to be a total communication breakdown.

They continue their discussion, and you observe. You don't know enough to suggest a structured situation at this point and thus don't want to exclude any possibilities. You observe them interact naturally, hoping to spot possible problem areas. (You can really do more than hope as we will see in the section on observation tools.)

Assume now that the same father and daughter asked you for help but were fairly specific about when the communication problem occurs.

"Our main disagreements are over my boyfriends and when and where I go with them," she states.

The father agrees that she has pinpointed the trouble spot. But even with this mutual understanding, unpleasant encounters continue to occur. In this instance, it would be appropriate for you to provide a structure, because you have some idea of what you want to observe. You might suggest, for example, that the pair role play a scene in which the girl is telling her father that she is going some place with a boyfriend. To be most useful, they should build the exercise around a particular boy and a specific place about which they have argued in the past. Or, you might play the role of a new boyfriend and have the girl introduce you to her father. The point is that since you have at least a tentative idea of the problem area, you can structure a situation which will provide relevant behavior for observation.

Another difference between unstructured and structured observation concerns the extent to which the behavior you observe is natural. In structured situations the people know they are generating behavior and can, if they wish, hold back or tone down extreme behavior which may be more typical of what they usually do. One simply has to weigh this against the advantages of structured observation.

Indirect observation, the third condition listed, is used frequently, but has its limitations. Often as a helper you don't have the opportunity to make direct observations of the troublesome behavior. You must make do with someone else's description of it. Thus, it is hearsay, or filtered indirectly into your head through the perceptual system of another person. Often you have no practical choice but to depend upon indirect observation. For example, when Dad comes in the door after work, and Mom says, "You've got to talk with that boy. He disobeyed me again and it's got to stop," there's probably no way that Dad can make direct observations. (He might try to set up a structured direct observation situation, but in this case that has its obvious limitations.) In many situations you must resort to someone else's description of what happened. If you are to try to help, one option, of course, is to postpone helping until you can directly observe relevant behavior. That can be the wisest decision when you are given conflicting observations of what has taken place.

The importance of paying attention to observation conditions is that they influence the effectiveness of the behavior observation and description tools. The context in which you do behavior observation, and the conditions under which you describe what you observe can be extremely important.

BEHAVIOR OBSERVATION TOOLS

How skillful is the average person at observing? One mother knows by the look on her child's face that the youngster is upset; another is oblivious to her child's unhappiness until the child demands attention. One office supervisor can walk into the workroom and accurately assess the negative human relations climate while another is unaware of the prevailing mood until confronted with a personnel problem. One hostess can accurately monitor how comfortable each of her guests is, while it never occurs to another that some of those present are uncomfortable. In other words, for some people effective behavior observation seems easy. Even though some of us develop more effective observation skills than others, one can learn to be a skilled observer.

We once had a teacher colleague who was an especially good observer. The dean of the department in which this colleague worked had a habit of leaving the office about three each afternoon. Sometimes the dean stayed on campus, and returned to his office around 5 P.M. before leaving for home. Other afternoons he would not return. Our colleague also liked to finish his campus work by midafternoon and leave for home. However, he believed that the dean expected most professors to be available throughout most afternoons. The interesting point in all of this was our colleague's uncanny ability to predict which afternoons the dean would return and on which the dean would leave for good at 3 P.M. In the latter occasions our friend would make an exit shortly after the dean's; in the former the professor remained clearly visible. We always wondered how he knew. The answer, some of us eventually discovered, was his skill of observation. Over the years he had discovered that when the dean departed for the day, the dean turned the page on the desk calendar to the next day. The dean did this only when leaving for good. The dean's office was situated in such a way that it was a simple matter for our colleague to glance at the dean's calendar each day after the midafternoon departure to determine whether the coast was clear!

The point of the story is that one of the most important considerations of effective observation is clarity of purpose. What do you want to learn from your observations? To which of the many specific behavioral patterns should you pay attention?

In this section we will describe three observation tools. These tools are in effect three different frames of reference from which you can make some kind of helpful sense out of human behavior. They are:

Communication process observation: The helper observes some relatively simple aspects of communication—who talks to whom and how much.

Determining goal-related behavior: The helper focuses on behavioral patterns which facilitate and detract from people's goals.

Role functions: The helper uses a standard set of "social roles" to identify who is doing what to whom.

Communication Process Observation

The first, and probably easiest to use of the tools, is *communication process analysis.* Essentially, that's jargon for "counting how much they talk and who they talk to." It's actually more than that, and complex systems for analyzing the frequency and direction of communication have been developed by people doing research in communication. For our purpose, however, a few basic skills should suffice.

You can use communication process observation to promote effective communication. Illustrative situations would include helping two employees resolve a conflict, assisting children, or parents and children to resolve an issue, and aiding a larger group such as a staff meeting or club discussion. One of the most basic considerations of communication is the relative amount each person speaks. Communication problems can occur when people dominate a discussion, withdraw, interrupt, or initiate private conversations. One often has a general impression of these kinds of communication barriers. Being more specific about your observations can be a more effective basis for helping improve communication.

There are two aspects of communication that you can learn to observe with relatively little practice. These are amount of talk (frequency of statements) and patterns of communication.

When two or more people are communicating, the simplest kind of observation is to note the relative frequency of remarks. You can note mentally, or even better, tally on paper, the number of remarks each person makes in a given conversation. Imagine you are observing three employees attempting to resolve an issue. After ten minutes you might have recorded seven marks for John, sixteen for Harry, and two for Joan. Harry is apparently dominating the conversation. This may or may not be inappropriate, but it should be helpful at least for the communicators to be aware of the fact.

Sometimes it is important to know more than the number of statements each person makes. Statements vary tremendously in length and content. A more precise way of observing the quantity of verbal participation is to use a given time interval. This consists of tallying at given intervals, every ten seconds for example, which person in a group is talking. List the names of the people in the group you are observing and then after each ten-second interval, place a tally mark next to the person who is speaking at that instant. To illustrate, imagine you have tallied a ten-minute discussion between five members of a committee which is having difficulty agreeing upon a policy statement for their organization. Your tally might look as follows:

Mike ~~IIII~~ ~~IIII~~ ~~IIII~~ ~~IIII~~ I	(21)	(35%)
Jean ~~IIII~~ IIII	(09)	(15%)
Carol III	(03)	(05%)
Mary II	(02)	(03%)
Bill ~~IIII~~ ~~IIII~~ ~~IIII~~ ~~IIII~~ ~~IIII~~	(25)	(42%)
Total	60	100%

Obviously, Mike and Bill are dominating the discussion. If Mary and Carol have anything to say, chances are that they did not make their contribution during the ten minutes observed. Again, there is no reason why everyone in a meeting should take up equal amounts of the conversation time. But when imbalances such as that just illustrated exist, it is often helpful for the group to have their behavior described to them.

Observing patterns of conversation, or who talks to whom, can also facilitate communication. Are people speaking to the total group or are remarks directed at one or two individuals? For example, Mary may direct most of her remarks to Joe because she thinks he will approve what she says. Bill may direct his remarks to Joe because he believes that he must "win over" Joe. In a group as large as eight or ten people, another pattern to look for is subgrouping. If Helen and Sally are conversing primarily with one another, while the other six people in the group are focusing on a common exchange, then something is probably amiss. Helen and Sally may be bored or preoccupied, feel excluded, or simply not interested. Even if it's the latter, their subgrouping doesn't help the main communication efforts, and more than likely is distracting to others. Making such an observation and reporting it to the group paves the way for improving what may be a faulty communication process.

Another important aspect which you can observe in group communication is "interruptions." Who interrupts whom, and how often? By observing interruptive behavior the "power structure" of the group can usually be detected. For example, one rarely interrupts the boss, but the person with power often feels free to interrupt others.

You can do communication process observation very informally, without others knowing that you are making a systematic observation. Often this is effective. For example, you may be attempting to help your coworkers resolve an issue. After informally observing their discussion, you might *mentally* note:

> Mary will often initiate the topic; and John makes short responses to her longer statements, often interrupting her. Typically, Mary talks twice or three times as much as John. John normally makes the last comment on a topic and nonverbally communicates that discussion is closed.

The information gathered by this observation allows you to make accurate descriptions instead of vague comments which may appear to be evaluative to others. Description skills are discussed in the next section.

Many group situations in which a task or goal is involved can benefit from someone being a communication observer. Meeting of community groups (e.g., PTAs, Planned Parenthood, League of Women Voters), church committees, planning groups, civic organizations, and staffs are examples of situations which can benefit from communication observation. Leaders of such groups can do communication observation themselves and they can ask members to do it. Also, as a member of a group, you can suggest that someone be asked to serve as an observer.

In all situations, the more specific your observations the more effective your behavior descriptions are likely to be. A report which starts, "It seems to me that . . ." is an opinion, and can be dismissed as such. But a report beginning, "During the last ten minutes the percentage of all remarks directed at John was . . ." is an objective statement regarding the group's communication.

Observing Goal-related Behavior

Another observation tool is goal-behavior observation. Most, if not all, human interaction is purposeful—that is, people have goals or objectives in mind. Their behavior is, in part, an attempt to reach their goals. When our behavior appears to be ineffective—when we seem to be no closer to the goal than when we started—we may become angry, frustrated, disappointed, despondent, or depressed.

There are many reasons people fail to attain goals. The goals may be in fact unrealistic, so vaguely defined that they are really nongoals, or there simply may be a lack of sufficient motivation to work towards the goals.

Another reason why people fail to obtain goals is that they are distracted by conflicting goals. We all have many goals and some are incompatible with others. People sometimes need help in seeing inconsistencies and deciding upon goal priorities. If your goal is to catch your limit of trout, then minding your own line ought to take precedence over pursuing the goal of keeping your kids happy by baiting their hooks and going back to shore for candy and pop.

Observing goal-related behavior consists of first identifying a person's goal(s) and then looking for behavioral patterns which facilitate and detract from that goal. Consider the following example of goal-behavior observation involving indirect observation. A mother, father, their fourteen-year-old daughter, Julia, and twelve-year-old son, Danny, are discussing privacy. Julia has accused Danny of taking money and magazines from her room. Danny denies taking the money but maintains that he has every right to enter his sister's room and borrow magazines. The mother is attempting to lecture Danny about honesty, and at the same time expressing her own disappointment at his behavior. The father is attempting to calm Julia while he also tries to ascertain whether or not her accusation is true. Tempers and voices get hotter and louder, tears begin to come, Danny swears at his mother, the mother insists to the father that Danny be punished immediately for using bad language, and the father stomps out of the house and slams the door shut behind him.

Imagine that you know the father and that when you meet him next morning he looks very discouraged. "What's wrong?" you ask, and he describes the happenings of the preceding evening:

> "It's worse than that," he continues. "Every time we try to discuss a family problem we get into a shouting match. I wish I knew what we do wrong. There must be some way to have a productive discussion."

Could you offer him any help? Here is how you might proceed, using the goal-related behavior observation tool.

First you could ask for a more detailed description of the episode. In this case we must make do with indirect observation of behavior. We would encourage him to be specific, and try to tell us what each person was doing and to avoid value judgments.

Following his description, the conversation might go as follows:

> "Bill, (the father), let's assume you are the one who will be responsible for promoting better discussions."
> "Okay."

"Now, what was your main purpose last night? Did you have a goal for the discussion?"

"Sure, I wanted to get to the bottom of things and see that it doesn't happen again."

"What do you mean by 'bottom of things'?"

"Find out what actually happened. Did Danny take anything from Julia's room?"

"Your first goal then was to establish the facts."

"Not just that. I also wanted to see that it doesn't happen again."

"What if it turns out that Danny didn't take anything from Julia's room— that nothing happened in the first place?"

"Well, then to be sure that he stays out of her room in the future. I don't see how you can separate one goal from the other."

"And you were trying to accomplish both at the same time?"

"Right."

We would now think something like the following to ourselves. We have a situation in which there were several goals including (1) daughter wanted brother punished, (2) daughter wanted assurance that brother would stay out of her room in the future, (3) mother wanted reassurance that her son was not really dishonest, (4) mother wanted father to punish son for bad language used during discussion, (5) father wanted to know whether accusation was true, and (6) father wanted to keep similar instances from happening in the future.

The people involved were trying to achieve several goals at various times during the interaction. Attention directed at some of these goals detracted from achieving others (punishing the boy versus getting at the truth). Some of the goals were not related, that is, achieving one would not necessarily contribute to the other (e.g., getting at the truth versus avoiding future incidents.).

We would then speculate to ourselves that if the father could decide which of his goals was most important, and recognize that much of his own behavior was not contributing to achieving that goal, then he would be in a better position to help the family move toward the desired goals.

We made certain observations which could serve as a basis for describing behavior to the father. We were able to do this because we have decided what we were trying to observe. Specifically, once the father stated his goal we looked for behavioral patterns which would tend to both promote and inhibit achieving them. According to his description, his efforts to "get at the truth" were obstructing "establishing a guideline for future behavior"— that is, the boy staying out of his sister's room. Had we been talking to the mother, we would have followed a similar procedure. We would have attempted to identify her goals so that we knew what behavior to observe.

Observing Role Functions

Roles refer to functions performed. Roles are a useful frame of reference for observing the dynamics of communication, in the sense of "who is contributing what" to the communication process. For example, one might describe the efforts of a skull crew in terms of the roles they play. The coxman plays the role of leader, the crew the roles of workers, and the one laggard preoccupied with showing off to his girlfriend on shore, the role of an inhibitor.

People who study communication have identified a large variety of roles that can be observed. We will consider three kinds of roles: task roles, maintenance roles, and self-oriented roles. Each is defined below.

Task roles People who assume a task-oriented role are chiefly concerned with "getting the job done." Their main interest is to accomplish the task the group has identified. Examples of task role activities include seeking and giving information and opinions (e.g., the moderator who gives his own opinions and asks for other's opinions), initiating activity (e.g., a scout leader who calls the youth to start the camping tasks), and summarizing what has been said or done. For instance, a husband and wife are discussing their budget and are trying to come up with a plan to cut expenses by $100 a month. They have been listing various types of expenditures when the husband comments on the high rate of inflation. He continues to comment on the current administration's contributions to high prices. The wife, assuming a task role, focuses on the purpose of their conversation, smiles and asks, "What items have we left out?" She is not rude, but chooses to keep the pair on their original task rather than engage in what could be another interesting exchange.

Maintenance roles When people assume a maintenance role their purpose is to make sure that the communication continues; that is, their concern is with maintaining or strengthening the interpersonal relationship between the people involved. People assuming maintenance roles are more concerned with a group's getting along well than with doing the task. Examples of maintenance role behavior include encouragement, acceptance, and helping in the expression of feelings.

Follow the husband and wife introduced in the task role seen above. Assume that the husband becomes discouraged and concludes, "It's no use. We just can't cut down on expenses." If the wife said something like, "It's discouraging, isn't it? But, we are making some progress," she would be playing a maintenance role.

Self-oriented roles When people assume a self-oriented role they are more concerned with a personal interest than with the purpose of others.

Examples of self-oriented roles include being overly aggressive, seeking attention and sympathy, not listening to others, and completely withdrawing from a situation. A person playing a self-oriented role in one way or another places personal needs above the concern of the group. To the extent that the person is successful in directing the efforts of the group to his or her agenda, group communication and accomplishments are inhibited.

Continuing the example, if the husband began to point out how many sacrifices he makes, he would be assuming a self-oriented role by diverting attention away from solving the common problem by focusing on his personal concerns.

Both task and maintenance roles make important contributions. Communication without both is likely to be less productive than when both operate. A totally task-oriented group may become so preoccupied with issues that it fails to consider the important subtleties of communication, thus failing to achieve its objective. A labor-management committee meeting has just been called to negotiate a labor dispute. The group had just been formed. The management members have all participated in negotiations before. The union members, however, are inexperienced. The situation is somewhat threatening to them. The management people take a hardheaded, "down to business," task-oriented approach. In the course of the conversation, the union people make several suggestions. Even though the management chairperson hears these, and even thinks they are useful, no comment one way or the other is made. As the meeting continues, union members stop responding. The chairperson is confused. "Aren't these people interested? Don't they have anything to contribute?" Not really. The group's problem was that no one was playing a maintenance role. The communication process had been ignored. Acknowledging the union people's contribution, checking perceptions, and attempting to clarify would be appropriate tools to use when one is playing a maintenance role.

At the opposite extreme, when everyone in a group is emphasizing maintenance functions, they may all feel very good about one another but may never accomplish their task. A balance between task roles and maintenance roles is ideal. How does one observe roles? Essentially by noting task, maintenance, and self-oriented behavior and the effects each has on people. Look for over-emphasis and absence of maintenance and task roles. Note when people assume self-oriented roles.

What you do with your observations will depend on your situation. If you are an acknowledged observer, then you will probably want to describe your observations to the group. If, on the other hand, you are a member of the group then you may want to use your information as a basis for changing your own behavior; that is, become more maintenance or task oriented, whichever seems to be needed.

The point we are making is that sometimes in order to be helpful we need to assume a role which is not usual for us. For example, a father usually provided the task orientation in family discussions. His aim was to get at the facts and come to a decision as quickly as possible. He assumed that all members of the family felt as secure about stating their points of view as he did about stating his. As his children grew into adolescence he became increasingly aware that fewer and fewer issues were being resolved via the family discussion route. There always seemed to be exceptions made following decisions. Someone would usually have a reason for not doing what the father thought had been the agreement. He mentioned his concern to his wife, who agreed with his perception. She also suggested that he was making it difficult for the children to express their real concerns and opinions. She added that if he wanted to know where they stood during discussions rather than discover it afterwards, he could show patience and interest in what they had to say. She was suggesting, in other words, that during family discussions he should put more emphasis on a maintenance role. He did, in ensuing discussions, and found that opinions and interest diverged more than he had assumed they would. As a result, problems became more difficult to resolve, but once reached, resolutions were more acceptable and lasting. The mother's observation and description about his role was very helpful to the father.

You may develop other role definitions which aid you to more effectively observe behavior. Remember, however, that roles should not become labels or stereotypes. Their function is to provide you with a perspective for observing the behavior that is taking place.

The three tools just described can be used selectively. Whatever way you choose to observe behavior, your general purpose is to increase your understanding of what is happening. If imbalance of participation in a discussion seems to be the problem, for example, then observing communication frequency is probably the most appropriate tool to use. If someone seems to be engaging in self-defeating behavior, then a goal-related behavior observation would seem to be appropriate. If an interaction seems to be going nowhere, or people are uncomfortable, or attention wanders, then using the task, maintenance, self-oriented roles frame of reference may be the most helpful way to go. It may not. Then try a different approach to observation. The point to emphasize is having a clear idea of what you are looking for. Narrow it down based on some hunch about the nature of the problem.

BEHAVIOR DESCRIPTION TOOLS

The reason for observing behavior is to provide a basis for making helpful behavior descriptions. The most careful observations are of little help to others unless you can describe them effectively. Conversely, a carefully constructed behavior description will be pointless or even harmful if it is based on faulty observations.

This section describes the following three tools for reporting:

Feedback—you describe your observations of another's behavior and its significance.

Debriefing—you lead others to describe and assess the significance of their behavior.

Confrontation—you describe resistance or avoidance behavior you have observed.

Each tool has a somewhat different function, and can result in different outcomes. We all know that it feels different to be "asked" rather than "ordered" to do something; to be "corrected" rather than "scolded." Similarly, *how* you describe can be as important as *what* you describe. In the following discussion, examples of behavior description are coupled with behavior observation.

Feedback

Feedback is straightforward reporting. When you provide feedback, you describe the behavior you observed. Feedback does not involve evaluating or suggesting courses of action. Those receiving feedback may believe you are evaluating their behavior. When you report that Bill is doing 85 percent of the talking, for example, it may seem that you are also evaluating Bill. On the other hand, feedback can imply suggestions on issues needing attention. There is no attempt to coerce, demean, or criticize. Your objectivity can help those to whom you are providing feedback feel less defensive.

In the following example, one person uses feedback from direct observations. In this instance, the helper had been part of the interaction in which he had made observations.

Chuck and Larry have been friends and neighbors for years and have often talked to each other about personal concerns. Chuck had changed to a new job six months ago. One evening while the two men were having a beer together, Chuck said:

> "Boy, I don't understand. All the rest of the salesmen seem to be against me. In the staff meetings when I come up with a plan they're all against me.

My ideas aren't that bad—in fact, they're good! I can't understand it."

"Has it been that way since you started the job?" Larry asked.

"No, not at first. For the first couple of months or so they listened to me and I think they liked my ideas."

"I don't know if this relates, Chuck, but maybe they're responding to you like I used to. I've told you I feel you sometimes reject my ideas."

"Yeah, what does that have to do with it?" replied Chuck, somewhat defensively.

"Don't get uptight; as I've said, sometimes when we've planned to do something together, like build the fence, and I suggest a way to do it, you won't say you don't like my way, but you suggest a new plan. I used to get irritated at you until we straightened that out. I really thought you were bossy and bullheaded. I wonder if you do the same thing in the staff meetings."

"Probably. I usually don't say why I don't agree with ideas—I just come out with mine. Maybe I've alienated all of them."

Larry could easily give feedback to Chuck because of their friendship. He could clearly describe Chuck's behavior and as an objective friend, he could relate his experience with Chuck to how others might see him. This could be constructive feedback for Chuck. Note that Larry said clearly that he wasn't criticizing Chuck. He was simply trying to describe what he had observed. Calling the others' attention to what you are doing can help avoid getting a defensive reaction to feedback.

Consider another illustration of feedback based on direct observation, this time in a work situation. Dr. Glen, a dentist, had received several comments from patients regarding confusion in his reception office and misunderstandings regarding appointment times. He was concerned and made a point to observe Carol, the office receptionist on several occasions. He wanted to know what, if anything, Carol had been doing which might result in client dissatisfaction. He found several things. He asked Carol to meet with him privately in his office.

"Carol, you sometimes appear flustered, especially when the reception room is busy. I want to talk with you about it."

Carol looked somewhat apprehensive, and replied, "What do you mean? Sometimes it is confusing when we get especially busy."

"I know, and that's to be expected. But maybe I can help. I've made a point to watch during the last couple of weeks. Perhaps it would be helpful to tell you what I've seen."

"Okay, but I do try."

"I know and I really appreciate your good work. I'm only trying to help with this particular situation. Okay?"

"All right," Carol replied, seeming less apprehensive.

"For example, I noticed that when you are in the middle of doing book work or billings, you pay very little attention to incoming patients. On the other hand, when you aren't preoccupied, you always greet them and indicate how long they may have to wait. Similarly, when you are preoccupied, you are very short when making the next appointment. When you aren't preoccupied, you always talk with them and verbally confirm the date. Does that sound accurate?"

"Probably—but it is difficult to do two things at once."

"I understand and I guess it's a matter of priorities. In this case patient reception comes first. If there isn't time left to do the book work we'll simply get additional help, or rearrange work loads. Does that make sense?"

"Logically, it does—but I get frustrated when I get behind in the book work. But I understand your point, and I will try."

You can also use feedback to assist a group to deal with troublesome issues which it has been avoiding. For example, Joan was attending a staff meeting during which the sales manager, sales people, and secretaries were attempting to resolve certain procedural matters. Resolution would require the cooperation of all concerned. The meeting was dull and seemed to be going nowhere. After observing for twenty minutes, Joan asked if she could report her observations. With an obvious expression of both relief and hope, the manager encouraged her to do so:

> Most of us appear uncomfortable. We have been asked for ideas, but we only speak when the manager directs a question to us. The secretaries are huddled-up on one side of the room and the sales staff on the other. None of us are looking at each other. We're all looking at the boss. There has been some private conversation which has probably been distracting to some of us. Two of the secretaries have been fidgeting on their chairs, suggesting to me that they may have a point to make, but feel as if they shouldn't. In short, we have been asked to work as a group, but the manner in which we are behaving suggests to me that we may not believe that is a genuine invitation.

In this illustration Joan's feedback identified and described an issue to which the group needed to attend before it could effectively pursue its basic task.

As the examples illustrate, feedback can be both relatively formal and informal. It may or may not be requested. In general, feedback can be more helpful if you (1) provide it at a time and place free of distractions, or at the time when the observation is most pertinent, (2) describe specific behavior, (3) describe the effect of the behavior on others, and (4) allow ample opportunity for clarification.

Debriefing

Debriefing is a tool for helping people learn from their experiences. You as helper ask questions intended to help the other persons describe and analyze their own behavior. The questions you ask are based in part on your observations of the other persons. Obviously, the questions you choose to ask reflect your judgment about behavior which you believe the other persons can profitably examine.

Debriefing can be contrasted with briefing. When people are given pertinent information and instructions prior to an activity, they are briefed. Pilots, for example, are briefed before a flight. In the process of completing their flight, they have experiences from which they can develop new information. When they examine their experiences and clarify the new information following an activity, they are debriefed. Organized groups, such as athletic teams, sales organizations, and medical staffs, make extensive use of debriefing. As a helper, it can be a very useful tool for you in providing behavior description. Following an important sequence of behavior, the helper asks a series of questions intended to assist the other person to understand the effects of that behavior, the impact it has on others and the way it can influence future actions and experiences.

We noted in Chapter 2 that self-discovery is an effective way of learning. Not only is self-discovery often more interesting than being told about oneself, it can be much less threatening. Debriefing rests heavily on this idea.

The function of the helper in debriefing is to provide some direction through probes, act as a memory aid, and provide support for going through the debriefing process. One of the important things to do in debriefing is to overcome the urge to provide your own feedback; to tell it like you saw it and give advice. Debriefing can involve your very active participation. You may ask extensive questions and do much clarifying. There are other times when there is a good chance that the person you are assisting will not be aware of your contribution. You will have said little.

Consider the following example, in which debriefing is done following observation in a structured situation.

A counselor was meeting with the parents of a boy who had often had trouble at school. The parents acknowledged that much of the son's problems grew out of their own failure to deal effectively with his concerns. Each parent explained the problem, placing most of the blame on the other. The counselor suggested that they role play a situation, and then debrief it. The counselor took the role of the son. He produced a midterm grade report from school indicating that he was failing three out of five subjects. He also said that one or both parents were supposed to meet with his teachers during the next week.

The parents, playing themselves, were encouraged to deal with the situation, as they might if it were real.

After about ten minutes, the counselor suggested that they stop the role playing and examine what had taken place. Much of the conversation had been concerned with who should attend the parent-teacher conferences. The mother had contended that both should. The father had argued for various reasons that it should be the mother's responsibility, but had not stated flatly that he should not attend. The conversation continued:

"What was the central concern in that discussion?" the counselor asked.

"What to do about the kid's poor work," the father replied.

"I didn't see it that way," countered the mother. "Most of the time we were arguing about who should attend the teacher conference, or really why you shouldn't."

"But that's your job—I couldn't get off work anyway," he said.

"You could if you wanted to," the mother responded.

The counselor turned to the father and said, "Can you summarize our conversation?" The father provided a fairly accurate description.

"Now," the counselor continued, "do you mind describing how you felt about attending the parent-teacher conference during the role playing."

"Okay. I guess I didn't want to go."

"In order for us all to understand how arguments like this one develop, it would be useful to know if you had already made up your mind. Do you mind sharing that with us?"

"Yeah, I guess I knew from the start that I wasn't going. No way was I going to that conference."

"And what effect might that decision have had on the discussion?"

The father smiled, seeming somewhat embarrassed, and replied, "I get your message. The conversation was pointless from the start; nothing could come from it."

"Nothing?"

"Well, nothing positive. We did get mad at each other."

Through the role playing the parents had a concrete sample of a typical means by which they deal with issues of responsibilities for their son. As the debriefing continued, they acknowledged that the issue of responsibility had never been discussed openly and honestly. The father also acknowledged that typically he made decisions without revealing them to others. Others became confused. Note that in the debriefing the parents identified their problem, rather than having it fed back to them. There was no need to defend themselves against the counselor. He had not made accusations, but rather helped the parents learn from their own experience.

Another appropriate use of debriefing, for example, would be following a staff or committee meeting. The situation need not always be negative. For example, one women's club committee, which had for several weeks experienced problems sticking to its agenda, had an especially productive meeting. The chairwoman, perceiving that everyone was pleased with the meeting said as the agenda was completed:

"I sense most of us feel better about this meeting than others we have had."

She heard a general murmur of agreement from the group.

"Why not spend a few minutes to see if we can find out what was different?"

During the short debriefing several "differences" were identified. For example, one member who had become increasingly disillusioned with the committee reported that for the first time no one came late and interrupted a meeting in process. Another pointed out that the refreshments were served following the meeting rather than during a recess which was the usual procedure. A third noted that the meeting was scheduled for one hour instead of the usual hour and one-half. Other people made similar comments. Even though debriefing the meeting offered no cure-all, it did provide a basis for making certain changes in future meetings which might result in more productive and enjoyable gatherings.

Confrontation

Sometimes people who are trying to solve a problem behave in ways that are inconsistent with their objectives. They take actions that actually help defeat, rather than move toward, their goals. It can be helpful, in those situations, if someone confronts them with the realities of their behavior. When you, as helper, point out inconsistent or self-defeating behavior, you are using a tool called *confrontation.* Sometimes the term confrontation has a negative implication. People are not usually confronted with pleasant events but rather with behavior which is ineffective. Note that it is a person's problem-solving behavior or lack of it, rather than the problem itself for which confrontation is helpful.

Confrontation can be used to focus attention on rejection or avoidance. Confrontation, in essence, consists of pointing out to an individual or group what you perceive to be an inconsistency between what they want to accomplish and the way they are behaving.

Feedback and debriefing often come before confrontation. Feedback and debriefing are used to help clarify and deal with an issue. When an issue is especially difficult, threatening, or unpleasant, it is not uncommon for people to reject or ignore the information contained in feedback and debriefing.

If confrontation causes defensiveness and more avoidance, then it's not helpful. Skillfully used, confrontation is effective without causing defensiveness. To be effective without causing defensiveness, focus the confrontation on behavior and not on personal attributes.

For example, Candi, a high school student, claimed she wanted to raise her grades because she wanted to have a wider choice of colleges. Her mother supported this idea and the two women discussed ways of achieving it. Increased and systematic study time, avoiding late-night TV, and doing extra-credit assignments were all part of the new scheme. Within three weeks, however, the plan had been abandoned. Candi was disappointed and reviewed the situation again. This time they decided to make charts, keep daily records of Candi's behavior, and use a reward system. The revised approach worked for about five weeks before falling apart. A very discouraged Candi, displaying much self-pity, complained again to her mother:

> "I just have too much to do," she stated.
>
> "You mean that there is not time enough to study as much as you planned."
>
> "Yes, I've really got to have some other kinds of help, or get my assignments reduced."
>
> "Let's review last week," the mother suggested.
>
> "Oh, that wouldn't do any good," Candi replied. "I'm just overburdened."
>
> "How many nights did you watch the late movie, for instance?" her mother persisted.
>
> "I don't know—okay, two or three, yes three nights."
>
> "How many nights did you do some reading after school?"
>
> "Two, I guess."
>
> "Well look, Candi," her mother confronted, "you have a goal you say is important, you made some plans, and we even revised these. Now you claim that there is too much to do, that your plan won't work. But you also just pointed out that you really didn't follow it last week. Do you agree? You don't know whether or not it will work."
>
> "Yes," the girl admitted.
>
> "Well, then it may be a good idea to rethink your goal. Maybe it's not as important as you thought. It may take more self-discipline than you are willing to muster. But whatever the reason, is there any point in not working at your goal and also feeling bad about it?"

Note there is no accusation. The confrontation deals with the inconsistencies between Candi's goal and her behavior and focuses on the dissatisfying outcome. Her mother is saying, in effect, you are not dealing with what you said you want to deal with, and as a result are making yourself unhappy and needlessly burdening me with your concern.

The mother could have told the girl that she was lazy, wasn't applying herself, or accused her of not caring enough. That kind of name calling would not be very helpful.

Confrontation is often useful to help another person evaluate the amount of commitment they have to a particular goal. It is one thing to claim that we want to change, and another to invest the effort to bring about the change. The contradiction between continuing to state an aspiration but failing to behave in a manner necessary to achieve it, can cause a good deal of unnecessary unhappiness. When unrealistic goals become standards by which people evaluate themselves, they continually come up with negative self-evaluations. They forget or are unaware that goal standards were arbitrary to begin with. They were not imposed from the outside. People set goals, and thus people can change them.

Consider this illustration of confrontation being used to help resolve this kind of problem.

Ben was an insurance salesman who often stated that he wanted to be the sales leader in his office. His goal was never met. The discrepancy between the monthly figure he set with the sales manager and his actual sales was causing him a good deal of frustration and considerable embarrassment. He was becoming very tense at work and irritable at home. The manager became concerned and arranged to talk with Ben:

"Ben, you seem unhappy. Anything wrong?" asked the manager.

"Disappointed, I suppose. I've really set my sights on leading the staff in sales but I just can't seem to make it."

"Any ideas why, Ben?"

"I don't want to make excuses, Dale, but I really think it's partly a matter of luck and partly a matter of poor leads."

"Let's look at the poor leads idea, Ben. Can you give me an example?"

"Yeah, I think so. Last month both Charlie and Bill had additional sales leads from nine or ten of their regular clients. I had only one. It must be luck, you know, that they had the best leads in the first place. If I had their customers, I'd have the additional sales."

"You really think so?"

"Sure—why not?"

"Want to hear it from my point of view?"

"Sure."

"First, your sales record is adequate. If it weren't, we wouldn't keep you. Keep that in mind." (Feedback)

"Okay."

"Besides being an adequate salesman, you're also an unhappy guy. But, in part, it's your own doing. You regularly announce to the world that you're going to be the top salesman, but you never make it. And you're frustrated." (Feedback)

"Sure I am. But it's not my fault."

"Ben, think carefully. Do you really want to invest the time and energy and make the sacrifice required to be a top producer?"

"I think so—I work hard."

"Sure you do—but how do you spend your evenings and weekends?"

"I make a few calls, if that's what you mean."

"Sure. But what else do you do? What are your other interests?"

"I bowl some. Usually do some weekend camping or some sports thing with the family. I read a lot, take the wife to see a movie every week or so."

"And those things are important to you."

"Sure—or else I wouldn't do them."

"Are they more important than making more sales?"

"I don't know. I never thought of it that way."

"I think they must be. And that's fine with me—and the company. But compare the way you spend your time with the way Charlie and Bill spend theirs."

"What do you mean?"

"Both Charlie and Bill spend at least four nights a week making calls. They also spend a good part of each weekend entertaining customers and planning strategy for the coming week. In other words, selling is their chief if not their only interest. You're different. You've got other interests. Why not acknowledge that to yourself and recognize that if you want to pursue them you're just not going to be our top salesperson. In other words, why keep setting a standard for yourself that requires more sacrifice than you're willing to make?" (Confrontation)

"It makes sense, all right, but frankly, is that the way the company wants us to think?"

"It's true, we want everything we can get out of you. But in your case, we'll probably get more if you're a little more at peace with yourself. I'm not saying that you don't want to be top salesman—most everyone does—that's natural. But do you 'want to' bad enough to give up some other things of value?"

Emphasize description and avoid making accusations. The latter involves evaluations which are only likely to lead to defensiveness. While confrontations are usually unpleasant, they should be made within the context of the inconsistency between the person's own goals and behavior. That is, avoiding laying on from the outside. Confront with their concerns and behavior, not yours.

Confrontation is, in a manner of speaking, saying, "Hey, you said you wanted to deal with that problem, but you're not. Would it be helpful to consider why you're not doing what you say you want to do?"

There is no necessary one-to-one relationship between kinds of conditions, observation tools, and description tools. Nor are you likely to find "pure" uses of the tools. Nevertheless, you can conceptualize any instance of reporting behavior as consisting of at least one of each kind of condition, observation tool, and description tool. Clearly, you don't always simply observe and then report. More often you observe, report, observe further (including a person's reactions to what you have reported), report, and so forth. The value of thinking in terms of kinds of conditions and relatively specific tools is the purposefulness and specificity which they add to your helping behavior.

MORE ABOUT PERCEPTION

Differences in perceptions, while a source of pleasure in life, can also be troublesome. We would like to conclude with several comments regarding perception. Perception, or the way each of us views people, events, and objects, can differ a great deal. Many disputes and much unhappiness stems from people disagreeing about what they have observed. Our purpose is to provide ideas for understanding perceptual problems. Three kinds of perceptual problems are discussed. The first involves perceptions in which people don't distinguish *what they observe* from *their evaluations* of those observations. The second is *selective perception* and the third *misperception*. All three kinds of problems occur when people report different perceptions of the same event.

Perceptions, Values, and Judgment

What we observe and how we value what we observe are not the same, but the two are often confused. Clarifying the difference between observation and evaluation can help resolve some perception problems. If people can agree on what they observed, they needn't argue about that. We might say, for example, "The congressman is stupid," and you might disagree. In making that statement, we confused an observation with an evaluation. We can both agree on the congressman's voting record; that we can observe. What remains, then, is a difference in values. Many people will readily admit that such differences do exist and that each of us has a "right to our own values." When a distinction is not made between the observation and the evaluation of what has been observed, it is relatively easy to continue arguing about who's perception is correct because the observations (which may be similar) become confused with the values (which may be very different). If we can first agree that our observations are similar, then it is more likely that we can acknowledge that each person may evaluate them differently.

Watch while a couple leaves a party:

> Mary comments, "I thought Bill's behavior was obnoxious. He thinks that he's just a little more wise and witty than everyone else!"
>
> "Oh, I thought he was pretty funny, Mary," John replies. "He wasn't putting anyone down—and he enjoys taking it as much as he enjoys dishing it out."
>
> "But he really was obnoxious," countered Mary.

The discussion soon evolves into an unpleasant argument about their evaluation of Bill's observed behavior. An alternative way of dealing with the difference in perceptions would be to acknowledge that their observations were similar. They both observed Bill making jokes and wisecracks. No argument there. The difference is in regard to their evaluations of the appropriateness of his behavior. Mary and John allowed the trivial difference in the evaluative aspect of perception to ignite a general argument and spoil an evening. (We are not, by the way, suggesting that discussions of differing values be avoided, only that they be based on something substantive.)

Selective Perception

Another source of perceptual difficulty is *selective perception*. Selective perception occurs when we focus on only part of what could potentially be observed. Barbara and Joan attend the same movie. Barbara concentrates on the costumes and observes them to be technically superior. Joan pays especially close attention to the film editing which she sees as poorly done. Discussing the film later, they are surprised to find that they disagree on its merit.

One reason selective perception occurs is that there is simply too much going on for us to observe all of it. We can only take in so much, and so we miss part of the action. Another reason is that we may begin an observation with a particular set of beliefs, values, and attitudes and thus are predisposed or choose to be selective in our observation.

We have all experienced selective perception. Men and women attending events such as style shows, automobile shows, plays, or almost any event will frequently have different perceptions to report because of sexual stereotype conditioning. Workers and supervisors will tend to highlight different aspects of a problem, and parents and children will emphasize different parts of situations in their perceptions. When two or more people are selective in what they perceive (even if their underlying values are not opposed) human relation problems can result. In the case of difficulties arising from selective perceptions, people actually do make different observations. They don't "see" the same thing and until each can become aware of what the others observed and are reacting to, disagreement is likely to continue. Calling attention to the selective nature of the perceptions can be an effective way to resolve such difficulties.

Misperception

Misperception involves situations in which there is a correct perception, but in which the perceiver makes an error. The message doesn't come across.

You observed a person smile and thought the person was pleased with your work. You misperceived because the smile was intended as a sarcastic sign of disappointment. The perceiver's observation may be correct—that is one sees what is to be seen, but one's filtering system leads one to an invalid conclusion. There is a "correct perception" because one person has a message to communicate or an impression to create. When not corrected, a misperception can lead to circumstances and relationships very different from those intended.

The following situation illustrates misperception. Bill, a high school student, arrived home about 4 P.M. He was upset about a low grade on a test which he thought was unfair. He stomped into the kitchen, slammed his books down on the table, made a sandwich, and ignored his mother. He had hoped that such a display would evoke a sympathetic, "What's the matter, Bill?" from his Mom, and thus provide an opportunity to air his resentment. But it didn't.

Mom, as it happened, misperceived Bill's silence as a request for privacy, and went on about her business, believing that her lack of questioning was what Bill desired.

The silence only increased Bill's frustration and led him to complain:

> "Why don't you keep more stuff for after school snacks? We're out of lunch meat and somebody drank all the coke!"
> "Now that's not my problem. If you want food for after school, put it in a sack ahead of time and mark it. I've told you that before . . ."
> "But that's not fair . . ."

And so an unpleasant exchange occurred about an issue that would not have come up had the mother not misperceived the meaning of her son's behavior. Let us be quick to add that we are not faulting Mom! Ideally, her son could have given her a more direct indication of his desire, but he didn't. As is often the case in such situations, the person who has a desire about what he wants us to perceive doesn't provide sufficient information for us to "perceive correctly."

Conflicting perceptions seem to be involved in a great proportion of disagreements. Using these three kinds of perceptual problems as a check list can often pinpoint one source of disagreements. Suggesting that people are not disagreeing about events per se, but rather about evaluations regarding observations can often help calm a stormy disagreement.

SUMMARY

In this chapter we have considered several tools for observing and describing behavior. These included communication process observation, determining goal-related behavior, role functions, feedback, debriefing, and confrontation. We have stressed the notion that each tool is essentially a frame of reference for providing clarity to your helping behavior. We urge you to keep that in mind. As you practice using the tools, you will probably discover and develop variations of their use beyond those we have provided as illustrations. That would be most appropriate. A frame of reference is just that—a structure within which you can do many things.

EXERCISES

1   To practice communication observation and analysis, select a TV discussion show to observe ("Washington Week in Review," for example). Try to pick a show that has four to six people discussing a topic. Write each group member's name in the form below.

GROUP MEMBER	SPEAKING FREQUENCY	TOTAL
1		
2		
3		
4		
5		
6		

Observe a ten-minute segment of the program and put a tally in the middle column each time a group member speaks. Total the results at the end of ten minutes.

A second observation will focus on length of communication for each group member. Again write each group member's name.

GROUP MEMBER	SPEAKING FREQUENCY	TOTAL
1		
2		
3		
4		
5		
6		

You'll need a watch with a second hand for this segment of observing. Again use a ten-minute segment. This time put a tally in the middle column at each ten-second interval beside the group member who is speaking at that time. Total the results at the end of ten minutes.

Compare the information on the two forms. Do the results surprise you in any way? Often we feel one group member is withdrawn when, in fact, they contribute consistently but with succinct remarks. Did the "leader" of the group speak the most or longest? How might this information be useful to this group?

2 Select another TV show. It can be one of your sitcom favorites ("All in the Family" would be great). Read the description of task, maintenance, and self-oriented roles again (pages 114–116). Write the names of the major characters in the show below.

CHARACTER	TASK ROLE	MAINTENANCE ROLE	SELF-ORIENTED ROLE	CAN'T DECIDE
1				
2				
3				
4				
Total				

Take a 10-minute segment and after each character speaks, classify that interaction as task, maintenance, self-oriented, or can't decide. At the end of ten minutes look at your data. Which character was most task-oriented? Maintenance oriented? Self-oriented? If you did Archie Bunker, it's highly likely that Archie demonstrated a lot of self-oriented behavior! In fact, if we saw Archie doing a lot of maintenance behavior, we would say he's "out of character." Look at the totals for task, maintenance, and self-oriented roles. For a group to proceed effectively, a ratio of about 2:1 between task and maintenance roles is usually desirable, with a low count on self-oriented roles. How does your group stack up? If it is high on task roles, it might get the task completed but have unpleasant interpersonal relationships. If it's high on maintenance, it probably gets along well interpersonally but may never get its job done. If it is highest on self-oriented, it neither gets the job done nor do like one another! Again, analyze what your data tells you about this segment. What kinds of roles are missing or need emphasis to make a more effective group? Of course, if these roles were played consistently, there would be no situation comedy shows!

3 In discussing role behavior, people often say that their personalities lean toward task or maintenance behavior. What about you? Are you more task-oriented or maintenance-oriented? How would your best friends describe you? What would it be like to display the other role more frequently? That is, if you see yourself as task-oriented, what would it be like to be more maintenance-oriented? Let's see.

As an experiment, for one-half of a day play your opposite orientation in regard to roles. If you're usually task-oriented, be more maintenance-oriented for four hours and vice versa. Note the following in your journal:

How did you feel trying little-used behavioral patterns?

How did others react to you?

What was good about the experiment?

Do you think you'll try it again?

4 Debriefing is the practice of learning from past experience to change future behavior. Debriefing can be done in three steps.

1 Describe the incident or situation.

2 Analyze the situation. Ask yourself probing questions (e.g., What effect did my behavior have on the situation? Why did things turn out as they did?)

3 Give yourself mental guidelines for the future based on your increased understanding.

As practice, individually debrief at least four incidents during the next few days and write notes for yourself below for each debriefing situation.

STEPS IN DEBRIEFING	INCIDENT 1	INCIDENT 2	INCIDENT 3	INCIDENT 4
Describe				
Analyze				
Guidelines for Future				

What effect does debriefing have on your behavior? Consider making it a regular practice.

5 Oftentimes we wish we could confront a friend or loved one about a specific issue or an aspect of their behavior. This is your chance to think it through. First, list four to six close friends in the following squares. Then under their names list specific issues or behavior with which you would like to confront them.

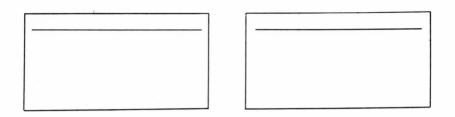

Are you surprised you had so many things to list? Now pick one of those issues or behavior that, in your opinion, if you confronted the other person, would in the long run improve your relationship. Of course, it's always risky to confront someone. Role play the confrontation. Now it's up to you. Will you do it for real?

6 Recall some recent times you've been given some helpful positive or negative feedback or been confronted with some aspect of your behavior. Briefly describe the helpful feedback and/or confrontation in the first column and note how it was given in the second column.

HELPFUL FEEDBACK	HOW WAS IT GIVEN?

Are there some common aspects to how the feedback was given (i.e., in an intimate setting, specific descriptions of the behavior, etc.)? From these situations can you describe the circumstances necessary for you to receive feedback most effectively.

7 At an upcoming meeting be an observer/reporter for a group. Ask the group's permission, then refrain from participation and observe some aspect of the group's process. Report your observations later in the meeting. Note your reactions to the experience.

How difficult was it to objectively report your observations to the group?
Did your perceptions of the group change by being an observer/reporter?

Seven | Resource Tools

This chapter provides you with information about community resources. Its purposes are to increase your awareness of the many helping resources, such as agencies and information sources, and to develop skills for directing people to them. Often the most effective kind of help you can provide for people with problems is to direct them toward appropriate helping resources.

To determine whether or not a resource will be useful, you must first identify the troublesome issue of the person who seeks your help. Effective communication tools, as described in Chapter 4, can be used by the helper to identify the problem(s). The concerns covered in this chapter include: children's problems, personal and family problems, educational decisions, financial planning, drug and alienation probelms, job decisions, legal problems, and physical disabilities. The chapter then describes resources which are probably available in your community or area to assist with each of the problem areas. Finally, the chapter will outline and illustrate the steps used in referring someone to a community resource.*

COMMUNITY RESOURCES

Finding the resource which can offer the most appropriate help to an individual can be a challenging problem. Two factors account for this. First, in most states there may be many agencies with resources to meet a particular kind of need. There is, in other words, no simple one-to-one relationship between problem and agency. Second, the complexity of procedures, juris-

---

*An annotated list of publications covering a variety of subjects is provided in Chapter 10. Each reference listed is aimed at a particular kind of problem or issue. All references are readily available and thus can be quick and valuable resources for your helping efforts.

dictions, and eligibility regulations regarding use of tax-supported, human resource agencies seems to mount each year.

Nevertheless, there are agencies and organizations which exist in one form or another throughout most areas of the country. Some are tax-supported, others are nonprofit, and still others are operated on a volunteer basis. They provide a variety of services aimed at relatively common problems. Some are directly available to private citizens, while the services of others may be obtained only by going through a standard referral procedure. In the remainder of this section we provide a brief description of the kinds of agencies and organizations which you as a helper can use when providing help with interpersonal, developmental, and educational problems.

Children's Problems

Kids with "hang-ups," be they physical or emotional, are probably most distressing, both to helpers and to the family needing help. Usually children cannot help themselves, and all too often those adults responsible for them are unable to be of assistance, due to ignorance, inadequacy, or fear.

State governments have taken some tentative steps toward recognizing the plight of these young people, and have established a variety of services aimed at meeting their special needs. State agencies have a variety of titles, but often are called *children's services division* or *division of child and youth services.* You can contact these by phoning the general number for the state government. On the local level, you can contact school district guidance departments which provide help for children and youth who have school-related problems. The problems range from physical and mental handicaps, through family dysfunction, to vocational and educational indecision. Elementary or high school counselors and principals are usually the appropriate people to whom inquiries regarding such resources should be made.

Personal and Family Counseling

An increasing number of communities are establishing mental health clinics. Most clinics provide individual counseling on an ability-to-pay basis. They are prepared to help with a variety of problems including those associated with alcoholism, personal relationships, and crises such as suicide, child abuse, and spouse beating. Some counseling agencies have crisis services and will respond to severe cases immediately. Many communities have agencies designed to help families resolve interpersonal problems. Such agencies have titles such as *family service agencies* or *family counseling services.* They also may provide individual counseling. These agencies are normally staffed by professionally trained counselors, social workers, and psychologists. They usually try to provide service to anyone who requests help, regardless of their ability to pay for services. They are listed in the yellow pages under counseling.

Tax-sponsored, public welfare offices exist in every state. In addition to providing funds to the needy, they provide a variety of other services related to family-centered problems. They may be labeled human resource division or adult services. Look in the phone book under the name of your city, county, or state.

Higher Education Opportunities

Entering and finding one's way through the world of post-secondary education can be a confusing and frustrating task. People attempting to make decisions and plans about post high school education and training need specific information regarding alternatives and procedures. Fortunately there are two sources to which one can turn in many communities for such information; namely, educational counselors and libraries. Most high schools and community college counselors have current information about local, regional, and sometimes national educational opportunities and needs. Schools, colleges, and often local public libraries also maintain educational information collections. The information you can usually obtain from these two sources are noted in the following paragraphs. (See Chapter 10 for specific references for most of the topics.) These resources should be helpful to a variety of people including young people looking for post high school educational opportunities, adults interested in occupational retraining or additional training, and individuals simply wanting more education.

College directories   The catalogs published by colleges are the most detailed source of information about particular schools. Catalogs can be obtained by writing to the admissions offices of the colleges in question. Most college libraries and many public libraries have collections of college catalogs. There are also a number of college directories which are a very useful source of summary information for comparing colleges.

College entrance testing   Many colleges and universities require or recommend entrance examinations. Students should check the entrance requirements of specific colleges to determine if such tests are required.

Two major national programs are available—those of the College Entrance Examination Board and the American College Testing Program. In most cases students take these tests in their senior year. Tests in the College Entrance Examination Board program are usually given locally in November, December, January, March, May, and July on specified Saturdays.

American College Testing Program tests are usually given locally in October, December, and February. Months may vary from year to year. School counselors have bulletins for both tests which provide detailed information and application procedures.

The College Entrance Examination Board also sponsors the *Preliminary Scholastic Aptitude Test* which college-bound students may take in October of their junior year for guidance purposes. The PSAT is a shortened version of the CEEB Scholastic Aptitude Test and gives students some experience with national testing programs and provides test data for early college planning.

College admissions services   A number of college admissions services are available for students who may have some difficulty in gaining college admission and who wish to have their credentials considered by a number of accredited colleges.

Scholarship and financial aid information   There are many sources of financial aid available to college students. Three of the chief sources are scholarships, loans, and part-time employment. Many schools have "packaged aid" programs which combine several kinds of assistance and are granted on a financial-need basis. Most colleges have written descriptions of their financial-aid programs. Write to the financial aid office of the school in question.

Many colleges use the College Scholarship Service. The service requires parents to file a confidential statement of financial resources and commitments. The service determines the financial-need level of the student and makes this evaluation (not the family financial statement) available to colleges to which the student applies for financial assistance. Contact a school counselor for information and application forms.

Vocational and Technical Education

Technical and vocational education is available for a multitude of subjects ranging from Art to Zen. Some of it is directed more at avocational than vocational interests, and meets important leisure-time needs. There are basically two sources of vocational-technical education; private and public.

Private vocational schools exist in every state. They are listed in the classified section of the telephone book under "schools." Most have catalogs and other printed descriptive information available for the asking. Most private schools are businesses and, as such, are interested in making a profit. Thus, they are generally more expensive than public vocational-technical education. Many state departments of education have available lists of private vocational schools.

By far the largest source of public vocational-technical education is the community college. In addition to their own vocational programs, community colleges frequently administer or coordinate special federally funded training programs and even company-sponsored–on-the-job training programs. Courses range from a few days to three years. An increasing number of community colleges are developing "open entrance courses." These courses are designed so that students can begin at any time (or at least more than once a semester) and proceed at their own rates of speed. Community colleges have descriptive materials describing their offerings. Most community colleges also employ counselors who are familiar with the colleges' resources and who can help plan educational programs which meet individual needs and fit individual circumstances. Finally, it is useful to know that some community colleges will provide specific short-term training programs when requested by a sufficient number of people.

Alternatives to High School Graduation

It is possible to complete high school graduation requirements by means other than regular attendance at a traditional high school. Some high schools have work-study programs in which students spend part of each day receiving on-the-job training through regular paid employment and also receive credits towards graduation for their supervised work experience. An increasing number of high schools have cooperative arrangements with community colleges by which students receive credit towards high school graduation by attending community colleges. There is also a program which leads to the General Education Development Certificate (GED). The GED Certificate is equivalent to a high school certificate of graduation (diploma). Both high school and community college counselors have information regarding these and other alternatives to traditional high school graduation.

Financial Planning

Families (and individuals) who are up to their ears in debt frequently lack money-management skills, Others, who may have the skills, are overextended due to some crisis, or simply because they lack the internal motivations to live within their means. One of the important services provided by most credit unions is financial planning assistance. Services differ among credit unions, but in general they offer help in analyzing spending habits, building budgets, and establishing savings programs. Some are even willing to take over a family income, make payment agreements with creditors, and disburse funds each month. People with financial problems can be referred to a credit union where they can explain their circumstances to an officer, who in turn will be able to indicate how the union can be helpful.

Drugs and Family Alienation

During the last few years free clinics and centers have appeared in many communities. Three of their chief concerns are offering assistance with drug abuse, youth alienated from their families, and crises.

The nature and quality of services offered by these clinics vary greatly. It is impossible to make a valid general statement regarding their value. Many are purely a product of the street culture. Others got their start from the street culture but now include professionals from the establishment. In any event, they can in many instances provide human resources otherwise unavailable. They represent the only place that some troubled youth will go for help. Sometimes they are able to assist in establishing communication between a youth and a family alienated from each other, and thus clear the way for an effective resolution of their differences. There are similar "organizations" in some communities which focus primarily on providing physical and psychological shelter for runaways. There are several ways to identify free clinics. They may be listed in the phone book under "counselors" or "psychologists." The local police department will usually know of their existence. Simplest of all, ask a youth you know if such an organization exists.

Many adults are suspicious of free clinics, believing that they encourage drug use, reinforce alienation, and otherwise contribute to "making matters worse than they are." In some instances they may be correct. In part, the validity of this point of view depends on our definition of "worse." Others find the free clinics difficult to accept because they know little about them, and are made uncomfortable by the problems with which they are concerned. This is understandable. Nevertheless, the helper who finds himself dealing with youth and family alienation problems of one shape or another should not discount a free clinic as a resource without first evaluating what it has to offer.

Job Choice and Placement

The problem of job choice can occur a number of times in one's lifetime. To a considerable extent the resource most appropriate to help in the job choice and placement process will differ according to one's current situation. For high school students deciding upon a first job, the high school counselor can be a good source. Many counselors have up-to-date information on local job needs and are often in contact with local employers. Some school systems are also becoming equipped to facilitate job choice and placement by utilizing computers which assist in matching students' interests and abilities with local, regional, and national job market data. The state employment offices operated by every state in the union are an obvious source.

College seniors and graduate students may have available the services of a career planning and placement office which assists by providing current occupational and labor market information; bringing business, government, and educational recruiters to campus; sending placement credentials to prospective employers; and training in job-search and interview strategies. College placement offices usually serve alumni.

Special job choice and placement problems are faced by some people. For example, middle-aged women returning to work, ghetto blacks with limited work history, a handicapped person who must be retrained, and the middle-aged "established" man who is phased out of his high-paying job, all illustrate special placement problems. The solutions might be a combination of personal counseling, vocational retraining, and learning new coping behaviors. State employment services would be appropriate agencies to refer each of these individuals. These agencies offer a wide range of services in vocational assessment and job counseling and placement, and they are also aware of other agencies in the community that might be an appropriate referral for a job choice-placement concern. State employment agencies also administer a variety of federal job programs. Many cities now have women's centers designed to assist women assess their life circumstances and to make transitions to different life styles. The orientations of women's centers range from counterculture to middle-class conservative. Some have professional counselors, others are staffed entirely by volunteers.

Legal Aid

Legal associations in many communities sponsor legal aid services. These services provide the assistance of an attorney to people who cannot afford to employ a lawyer. Legal aid societies limit their services to matters involving civil law, but may also be able to assist a person to obtain appropriate legal representation with regard to criminal law. For example, an individual uncertain about the legality of an act contemplated or uncertain about legal rights and responsibilities can obtain assistance from legal aid offices. Legal aid offices are usually in telephone directories. If not, contact your city or county district attorney's office for information.

Meaninglessness/Loneliness

Feelings of meaninglessness, helplessness, and loneliness can have both internal and external aspects. Self-perception may be the main problem. Consider a person who has what others see as an interesting job, but who actually feels lonely and without purpose.

There are several resources which can be used to help such people make human contact and engage in activities which they may find meaningful. Many communities have volunteer centers or volunteer services. These services match people who need something done for them with people who desire something to do. Volunteers assist in hospitals, convalescent homes, youth groups; provide transportation; read to the blind; perform typing; write letters; and many, many other things. From your perspective as a helper, the specific volunteer tasks are not as important as the opportunity for assisting another to engage in behavior which usually is already structured and ongoing. The volunteer does not need to do a lot of planning or arranging before starting. He need only "show up" and he is put to work.

Other sources of instant activity are community colleges, YMCAs, and adult education programs. Many adult courses are actually recreational activities which involve neither reading nor tests, and need not scare off people who have negative associations regarding schools. They offer potentially powerful resources for people wanting to associate with others who are searching for meaningful activities. School-based programs are less "instant" than volunteer work, but they do provide ready-made structure and content for the person who is having difficulty getting organized alone.

Physical Disabilities

Many people experience some kind of physical disability during their lives. Obviously, some people so affected have personal resources or insurance by which they can obtain needed medical and rehabilitation services. There are many others, however, who lack the extensive personal resources required to meet such needs.

Fortunately, there are several sources of public assistance available in rehabilitation with regard to children. Most states have tax-supported children's services divisions which provide direct rehabilitative and medical services as well as coordinate the use of other public resources (such as state medical school hospitals) for individual cases. Special education and guidance departments of public schools should be able to make initial contact with state-supported services for children's disabilities. With regard to adults with problems of physical disabilities, all fifty states have a vocational rehabilitation service. Any persons sixteen years or older with a disability which renders them unemployable are eligible to receive assistance. The mission of vocational rehabilitation services is to help such people become employable.

Sex Concerns

Sex has been given a lot of attention in the seventies. It is not that it hasn't been done before, but now we talk about it a lot. People want information and instructions regarding sex and reproduction.

There are many new resources to meet this growing demand. There are counselors and psychologists who specialize in sex counseling, and a number of universities have special treatment programs for sexual dysfunctions. There are also many written materials that can be helpful in expanding your knowledge of sex. Depending on whose opinion you value, you can ask a good friend, your minister, or your physician to give you recommendations for materials.

The information available goes beyond a concern for satisfying sexual experiences. Extensive information regarding abortion, fertility, family planning, genetic concerns, and birth control is available. Look in the yellow pages of your phone book under "birth control information center" or "family planning information." The important point is that people today need not be ignorant about sex and reproduction. Excellent information is readily available.

The availability and effectiveness of the kinds of human resources vary from community to community. Nevertheless, they do represent wide and useful resources readily available to you as a helper.

THE REFERRAL PROCESS

When the helper puts an individual in touch with a resource, the helper is using the referral process. The process involves several steps which allow the helper to assess whether a referral to a particular resource is appropriate and to estimate how much assistance the individual will need in order to gain access to the resource.

Before looking at the steps in the referral process, let's consider how a helper knows when a referral should be made. There are two main considerations. First is the helper's skill level. If the persons needing help have problems clearly beyond your ability to help, refer them.

The second consideration in referral concerns the helper's personal situation and feelings. If you feel that you don't have the time or energy to get involved, it is better to refer. Also, if you feel that you might not be objective, or for some other reason might not be an effective helper in the particular situation, refer. The points discussed in Chapter 3, i.e., confidentiality, authority, psychological closeness, commitment, and dependency, are all reasons why helpers might choose to refer.

If you have decided that a referral is appropriate, the following eight steps will help you identify resources and refer people to them:

1 Define the problem. What does the person seem to need? Can he or she tell you? If not, can you help identify the problem? What has been done so far?

2 Do you know of an appropriate resource? If not, are you willing to locate one?

3 Describe the resource, and indicate how it can be obtained.

4 Find out whether or not the individual is interested in using the resource.

5 Does the individual want help in proceeding?

6 If so, are you willing to provide help?

7 Determine your responsibility, if any. What will you do?

8 Follow through.

Most referrals are done much more casually than just suggested. Nevertheless, going through the steps mentally should improve the referral.

It should be emphasized that step 2 (Do you know of any appropriate resource?) involves several considerations. These include the accuracy of your information regarding the service available from the resource, the effectiveness of the resource, and, of course, the clarity of the needs of the other person involved. A flippant suggestion to use a resource which may in fact be highly inappropriate can be both discouraging and debilitating.

Following is an example which illustrates the referral process just described.

Mary Collier is a high school teacher. She stops to buy gas at her neighborhood station, and the following conversation takes place with Sam Collins, the manager, whom she has known for several years:

"Mrs. Collier, is there any way I could get you to help my kid, Bill, get a better program at school?" asked Sam.

"What's the trouble, Sam?"

"He's talking of quitting. Says its dull and too hard."

"What have you done so far?" Mrs. Collier asked.

"Nothing much. His mother was going to see some of the teachers, but she didn't."

"How do things stand with Bill?"

"I think he's been skipping a lot," his father replied. "Puts him in a bad light to ask for special help. But I think he'd really want to stay in school if it made more sense."

"So you think Bill may not be exactly received with open arms, but that he wants help?"

"That's about it," admitted Sam.

"Bill could see his counselor for help. Maybe the three of you could meet."

"What could he do?"

"The school is more flexible than many people think. The counselor could help Bill change to classes more interesting to him, or maybe get him in a program that involves more practical experiences."

"That sounds good. How do I go about it?" asked Sam.

"You can call the school for an appointment with Bill's counselor. Or if you'd like, I'll talk with the counselor and ask him to call you and set up a meeting."

"That sounds good."

"Okay, I'll see him in the morning and ask him to call you at work."

"Fine," said Sam.

"Do you think it would help to tell Bill about our conversation? It might be important to avoid surprising him, and also to let him know you are interested in his problem."

"I'll do that—I think he wants some help."

PROBLEMS OF REFERRAL

All referrals do not go as smoothly as the one described above. Difficulties do arise. In the previous example, Mrs. Collier's referral suggestions and actions were appropriate because she was asked for help, and the referral was part of her own profession. However, the limit of responsibility is not always clear and can be a problem. As a helper, you should decide where your responsibility regarding referral ends. In the previous example, Mrs. Collier identified the problem, described a resource, and also facilitated Sam's using the resource by offering to make the initial contact with the school counselor. She could have left this latter responsibility to Sam, but in this instance she thought that his lack of familiarity with the school and the counselor might inhibit his following through. If Sam had shown serious apprehension about approaching the counselor, Mrs. Collier might have gone even further and offered to meet Sam at the school and introduce him to the counselor. The important point is that Mrs. Collier determined the extent of her responsibility for the referral. She did not get herself into a situation in which other people were confused about her involvement.

Referrals can get clearly out of hand and result in bad feelings between you and the person being helped. One reason for this is the helpers' failures to make their intentions clear. They don't set limits or clarify the ground rules for helping.

To illustrate, consider a situation in which Alice refers her friend Joyce to a marriage counseling center. The referral process included Alice's helping Joyce clarify her concern, evaluating alternative counselors and services, and role playing the initial conversations with the counselor. Alice also tried to clarify that once Joyce had gone to the counselor, she should not continue to describe and otherwise involve Alice in her marriage problems. For several reasons, Alice felt it neither appropriate nor helpful to continue being a listener.

Apparently the first counseling meeting was satisfactory, and Joyce thanked Alice for "helping me take the important first step." About two weeks later, the two friends were having tea, and Joyce volunteered that the marriage counseling wasn't going too well:

> "It may be worth staying with it, nevertheless," Alice responded.
>
> "You can say that, but you haven't had to go through it. It's really irritating to be continually told how *I'm* the cause of many problems. That's not what I expected."
>
> "That's too bad."
>
> "I really think you might have suggested another counselor," Jane continued. "After all, it's not only unpleasant but expensive. You didn't tell me that it would cost so much."
>
> "Hey, wait a minute," Alice responded. "You're blaming me for your dissatisfaction with your counselor. That's not my doing. Remember that I helped you do only what you said you wanted. If you are unhappy with counseling, why don't you discuss it with the counselor?"

Alice may appear a little harsh, but if her intent is to stay out of Joyce's marital problems, then she probably should be. One way to continue to be helpful to her friend would be to point out that they can still remain friends, that she can be a person with whom Joyce can have some satisfying experiences precisely because Alice *is* uninvolved in a troubled area of Joyce's life.

The example of Alice and Joyce illustrates a classic problem in referrals; the person blaming you when the referral doesn't work. It's usually easier to lay blame at the helper's feet than to analyze why the referral is not effective from the individual's point of view. The best way to remedy this problem is to make it very clear when the referral is made that this may not resolve the problem or issue. If the persons seeking help understand this and choose to seek out the resource, they are more likely to take responsibility for the consequences of the referral.

Another problem of referral is the feeling of rejection. Often if a person has chosen to share a problem or concern with you, the last thing wanted is to be referred some place else. Some individuals feel you "let them down in their time of need" or that "you really don't care" if you send them some place else. This difficulty should be dealt with sensitively Through effective communications skills you can communicate why a referral is the most caring thing you can do for them.

There are difficulties in referral about which you, the helper, have little control. For example, it is possible that the person you refer to a counseling agency will be seen by a counselor-in-training who has not perfected his or her counseling skills. Or one might find that receiving help at an agency is contingent upon being a subject in a research project.

Other referral problems include cold and insensitive reception procedures, voluminous forms and paperwork, different value orientations, seemingly endless delays, and inefficiency. While you as a helper have no control over these difficulties, you can prepare the person you are helping to anticipate possible difficulties. The person can see that when the difficulties exist they are part of the price to be paid for the help. Obviously, some people won't be willing to pay the price of putting up with such inconveniences.

The best advice you can give in regard to referral sources is, "Let the consumer beware." Referral resources, as any other service, should be scrutinized. People should assess the kinds and quality of service available. Urge the person you refer to ask questions, such as:

What are your agency procedures?

What is your orientation to helping?

What are my rights as a client?

What are the fees?

How much time will it take?

What are the qualifications of staff?

These, and other questions, can be asked in a direct, but inoffensive, way. If the person you refer has a "consumer beware" attitude, they are much more likely to get what they want and need from referral resources.

The basic way to deal with problems of referral is to pay special attention to how and what you communicate to the person being referred. Be as clear as you can regarding what the person should do, what can be expected from the referral, and your involvement. Take time to check the individual's understanding of these considerations.

SUMMARY

The underlying concern of this chapter has been to make you aware of the many helping resources available in most communities. To use them appropriately and to best advantage, you must know what resources are available, and you must be skillful in putting those you would help in touch with them. Toward the first requirement, descriptions of various community services were provided. As an aid to improving referral skills, we described steps in the referral process. Additional and more specific resource tools are listed in Chapter 10.

EXERCISES

1 As an exercise in knowledge of your community, try the following. List below four concerns you have. In the right column list specific resources in the community to which you could go for help.

CONCERNS	POTENTIAL RESOURCES
1	
2	
3	
4	

Could you think of at least one resource for every concern? If not, ask others for their suggestions.

Are you currently using any of the resources? If not, what would it take (e.g., more information, a friend's encouragement, etc.) for you to avail yourself of the resource?

2 Most communities above 10,000 people have directories of community agencies. Does yours? To find out call the local mental health clinic, public library, or ask a local psychologist or physician. Look through the directory. Most list agencies by function (e.g., alcoholism, children's problems, etc.). If you don't find a directory, how might you encourage getting one started?

3 Most of us have had the experience of being referred to an agency or a specific person. The act of referring is a skill; and as you've probably experienced, some have it and some don't. List the last few times you've been referred and by whom. Then reread the eight steps of referral (p. 144) and note in the last column why the referral was effective or ineffective.

REFERRED TO	REFERRED BY	COMMENTS ON EFFECTIVENESS OF REFERRAL

4   Think of the last time you referred someone to a community resource. How effective were you? Compare what you did to the eight steps of referral? What might you change if you had it to do over again?
     What about the next time you refer? Think it through. Write your actions in your journal.

Eight | Helping Strategies

PURPOSES OF HELPING STRATEGIES

In Chapter 2, when we were discussing the various parts of the helping process, we noted the importance of strategies. A strategy is a plan for, approach to, or a method of proceeding. It involves your thinking about the tools and resources you will need, the extent to which other people will be involved, and the extent of commitment you are willing to make. Strategies have at least two purposes in regard to helping. First, when you have made an effort to plan you will probably gain a better understanding of what the individual you are helping is concerned about. Thinking about how you will help usually forces you to be more specific about what is concerning the other person. Before you can answer the question "How can I help Roger, who feels lonely because he has recently separated from his family?" you must be more specific. What time of day is Roger most in need of help? Why can't he cope with his feelings? What other resources does he have? As you answer these questions, you're gaining clearer understanding of Roger's problem. On the basis of this understanding, you should be in a better position to determine which helping tools are most appropriate and thus maximize the assistance you provide. The second advantage of developing helping strategies is to help you avoid wasting time with purposeless helping behavior.

We are not suggesting that you go to the war room and chart a course of action each time you become involved in a helping situation. We are asserting that in any more-than-simple helping situations your efforts will be more helpful if you consider your objectives as a helper, select your behavior purposefully, and determine the contraints on your role. This is really no different from any other situation in which you invest your time and energy. Having at least a general plan is assurance that *you* will be pleased with your efforts.

DEVELOPING HELPING STRATEGIES

This chapter describes and illustrates a five-step method for developing helping strategies. The method assumes that you have at least some of the helping tools discussed in prior chapters, and that you can identify constraints, such as time, relationships, and confidentiality, which operate in a given helping situation. The five steps are:

1 *Translate* into outcomes the problem of the person you are considering helping. Find out how "things are not as that person wants them to be" and try to learn what changes would need to take place in order for "things to be more like the individual wants them to be." The "things" are outcomes.

2 *Choose* the appropriate tools you could use to help achieve the outcomes stated in Step 1. Decide the order in which you would use the tools, if appropriate. This is your "tentative strategy."

3 *Consider* what possible constraints your underlying relationship may place on the helping effort and modify your tentative strategy, if appropriate. (The constraints of authority, confidentiality, commitment, psychological closeness, and dependency are discussed in Chapter 3.)

4 *Begin* the helping strategy.

5 *Maintain* an ongoing evaluation of your strategy and revise it, if appropriate. (The ongoing evaluation is concerned with both the appropriateness of your perceived outcomes and your strategy.)

We pointed out earlier that the components of helping consist of a problem, helping tools, and outcomes. The helping strategy puts it all together. Let's examine each of the five steps in greater detail.

Step 1: Translate the problem into desired outcomes Earlier we suggested that when some people state a problem or complaint they are in effect saying, "Things are not as I want them to be," and that when they can say, "Things have changed—they are more like I want them to be," they will have achieved desired outcomes. If they can describe the changes that would need to occur before desired outcomes are reached, they are probably ready to begin the helping process.

Frequently, people find it difficult to describe desired outcomes. Moving from a vague feeling of unhappiness to having a clear idea of "what is wrong" is often a major move towards solving a problem. The skillful use of the communication tools of active listening, i.e., acceptance, clarification, paraphrasing, perception checking and probing, can lead to clearer statements of both what is wrong and what are the desired outcomes. As noted in the discussion of active listening, helping people clarify their concerns and desires is often sufficient. The only assistance they desire or need is with clarification. In any event, understanding their concerns is the first step.

Consider John, a high school junior, who had appeared preoccupied. For a couple of weeks he had seemed "down" to his father:

> "What's the trouble, John?" his father asked one evening. "You seem sort of discouraged lately."
> "I am, Dad—don't know why."
> "No idea, huh?"
> "Well, yes, some—school I guess. I'll finish in another year, and I really haven't learned much. I'll have to do something, but it all seems so uncertain."

John's father encouraged him to talk more about his concerns. The father listened actively. Soon the father was able to translate John's general concern into what he heard John saying were possible desired outcomes. He suggested:

> "John, are you saying that you would like to have a better understanding of what options will be open to you after high school? And would it lessen your concern if you could develop at least a tentative plan for the near future?"
> His son replied with some enthusiasm, "Yes—that's the problem. That's what I need."

Given a more definitive statement of the problem, that is, having translated it into desired outcomes, John's father is now ready to plan a helping strategy with his son.

Helen was doing volunteer work in a convalescent home. One of her new patients was Mrs. Gordon, an older woman who had few visitors. Mrs. Gordon appeared to have difficulty making friends with other residents. Helen made a special effort to know Mrs. Gordon. Even though she believed she had gained Mrs. Gordon's confidence, she realized that the older woman continued to be inactive and alone.

One afternoon during a conversation Helen asked, "Mrs. Gordon, you don't seem very happy. Can you describe how you feel—is there a particular problem?"

Mrs. Gordon acknowledged that she was unhappy, but would say little more than that she was lonely.

This may appear to be a relatively concrete problem, one which could easily be translated into outcomes. Obviously people who are lonely need people around them. Or do they?

Helen didn't jump to that quick conclusion. Instead she encouraged Mrs. Gordon to talk about her interests and her life before coming to the convalescent home. During their conversation Helen learned that Mrs. Gordon wasn't especially people-oriented. Much of her time had been spent in solitary activities and she liked it that way. Currently there were several activities that she wanted to do, but while residing in the convalescent home she would need to be dependent upon other people to get sewing and craft supplies. But she said she couldn't stand being obligated to other people.

Helen thought she now understood the loneliness problem and could translate it into desired outcome.

> She said, "Mrs. Gordon, it's really not people, friends, and acquaintances that you need, is it? If you could learn to let other people assist you without resenting it, you would pick up many of your old activities."
>
> "I think you're right," replied Mrs. Gordon. "I just can't stand being beholden to anyone."

Given this desired change as an outcome statement, Helen could plan a helping strategy.

There are times, of course, when outcomes are not as easily identified as in the previous two examples. In such instances, clarification itself may be the first desired outcome of help, and a strategy leading to clarification is the first order of business. The process of clarification is described in Chapter 4, pp. 45–51.

Step 2: Choosing appropriate helping tools The helping tools you have already studied can be used in a number of combinations as you help people move towards desired outcomes. Follow John's father and Helen as they match tools with the desired outcomes.

John and his father had identified two outcomes: (1) a clearer understanding of options open to John following high school; and (2) a tentative plan for pursuing these. John's father then thought about which tools he could use to help John achieve the desired outcomes.

"In order to identify options, John probably needs a clear picture of his interests and abilities. I can use active listening to help him to do this. He knows several options, but I can probably fill in some details and suggest other sources of information. Active listening can be used to help him place some priorities on these. With regard to a plan, I can suggest a simple decision-making procedure. I can also verbally reinforce the planning effort."

John's outcomes were relatively easy to identify and achieve. The changes or tasks John faced did not conflict with an established value and the help from his father did not make him defensive. However, Mrs. Gordon's outcomes were more difficult for her to reach than John's were for him to reach. Change for Mrs. Gordon meant putting aside her need for independence, a cherished value. Helen is faced with helping Mrs. Gordon either modify a particular value (dependence), or helping her find means of accepting help from others without feeling beholden.

Helen considered two kinds of tools. First, she could use active listening to help Mrs. Gordon understand that different circumstances in her life might call for flexibility. Given a new understanding, Mrs. Gordon might be able to accept help and not resent being dependent upon others. An alternative Helen considered was a version of contracting. She, Helen, would help gather craft materials, for which Mrs. Gordon in turn would agree to make articles which Helen could use as gifts for Christmas and other occasions. By using the second strategy, there was no need to change Mrs. Gordon's values. As a helper, Helen could make it possible for Mrs. Gordon to behave consistent with her values in the new situation. There is a difference between rationalizing away one's values and being flexible in the light of changed circumstances. People sometimes find the distinction difficult to make. In this instance, Mrs. Gordon didn't abandon her desire to be independent, but made a reasonable accommodation in a particular situation. Helen helped her do this by providing an opportunity for Mrs. Gordon to pay her way.

Step 3: Consider constraints of the underlying relationship Completing Steps 1 and 2 results in a tentative strategy—one which would be ideal, everything else being equal. Often, however, there are constraints on the helping relationship. These constraints are associated with the underlying relationship with the person you are considering helping. These constraints are the five conditions of underlying relationships which can influence the nature of the help you can and want to provide. At the risk of oversimplification, we are suggesting that you can use these conditions to identify constraints which might exist, so that you can modify your tentative strategy accordingly.

The conditions of underlying relationships are displayed in Figure 2. Each of the five columns represents the condition indicated. Each row indicates the extent of constraints that the conditions might impose. To use the chart, first consider each condition in regard to a particular helping situation, and decide which degree of constraint applies. Second, modify your initial strategy accordingly.

Let's continue with John's father and Helen to illustrate how the constraints operate. In the case of John and his father, you will recall that the

	Authority	Confidentiality	Commitment	Psychological closeness	Dependency
1	None or not important	None	No limitations	Not an issue	Not an issue
2	Must be considered —could constrain	Exists and needs to be defined	Limited— must be considered	Could interfere	Could develop
3	Definitely a constraint	Definitely a constraint	Strong limitations	Prohibitive	Highly probable

Figure 2   Constraints of helping

father's tentative strategy was to do some active listening to help John clarify his interests and abilities, to provide information from his own experience regarding options, and to demonstrate a decision-making planning procedure. He would also reinforce the exploring planning behavior. The father reviewed this strategy from the perspective of the five conditions of the underlying father-son relationship. His thoughts were as follows:

> *Authority* might be a constraint. If I appear to be taking over, or directing John, he's liable to resist. Thus I'll do what I planned, but I'll be especially careful to let him set the pace. *Confidentiality* isn't important. It is a matter between the two of us, and it doesn't concern anyone else. I'm *committed* to helping John, and I'm willing to spend as much time helping John as he wants and needs. Thus I should be ready to put aside other activities when he wants to pursue this issue. I want to keep it informal, so I won't schedule time with him but let him know I'll make a contact if *he* wants or needs one. *Psychological closeness* is not a constraint. I'm concerned, but not preoccupied or overinvolved. John will ultimately make his own decisions and that's fine with me. Knowing John, I'm sure *dependency* isn't an issue. He wants to be independent.

After going through this brief exercise, the father did modify his tentative strategy in that he cautioned himself not to push, to let John take the lead. Had he not thought through the underlying relationship beforehand, he could have found himself pushing John, and John, in turn, might have resisted his help.

The example of Helen and Mrs. Gordon illustrates the influence of another kind of underlying relationship in helping strategies. In this instance Helen's relationship with Mrs. Gordon was strictly that of an interested volunteer worker. You will recall that she had identified two alternative strategies: (1) try to have Mrs. Gordon put aside one of her values to accommodate her new situation, or (2) help within the context of the existing values. She used the underlying relationship chart as a means of developing a strategy. Her thinking went as follows:

> There is no authority involved, nor is confidentiality a concern. Psychological closeness and dependency need not be a concern. However, commitment is important. My volunteer time is limited, and I suspect that the first alternative, changing her ideas about dependence, would be relatively time-consuming. I would probably need to do periodic follow-up reinforcing. The second alternative is relatively straightforward and clear-cut and would be less demanding of my time.

Step 4: Begin   Having modified the tentative strategy, if necessary, it is then implemented. In the example of John and his father, the father waited for an opportune time, and then indicated his interest in talking with John about the concern they had discussed earlier. In the second example, Helen suggested the contract approach as a way of helping Mrs. Gordon. They determined the materials that Mrs. Gordon required, and settled on her contribution.

Getting started, especially when the helping is to take place over a longer period of time, can be facilitated by having the person you are helping participate as you structure what is to take place. Structuring clarifies the relationship between your activities and the desired outcomes they have identified. In the example of John and his father, it could be useful for the father to review with John what was going to take place, and the purpose of the initial conversations about interests and abilities, especially if the father suspected that John might be wondering, "What's the point of all this talk?"

In many kinds of human activities structure, or predictability, is exactly what we don't want. The mystery and surprise in such activities makes them enjoyable. But by definition helping situations are usually problem-solving situations in which people are doing their utmost to generate purposeful behavior. Therefore, whatever we can do to clarify the purpose of the behavior is useful. Not letting them in on what is taking place, in most instances, smacks of game playing at least and is condescending at worst. Unfortunately, an example familiar to many of us can be drawn from the typical physician-patient relationship. The experience of consulting with a physician who won't tell us what he is going to do next, let alone what purpose he has in mind, not only can evoke frustration and anger, but equally important, can deter us from behaving in a cooperative, facilitating manner. Compare that experience with one in which the physician tells us ahead of time what is going to happen and even why, and our point should be obvious. Most helping situations are cooperative efforts between the person helping and those receiving help. To keep the latter in the dark regarding what is taking place, makes it difficult for them to be cooperative, to say the least.

Step 5: Maintain an ongoing evaluation and revise strategy when needed   This is not a difficult task if you pay attention to what is happening as a result of your helping efforts. You can both observe informally and ask the other person straight out if your efforts are helpful.

Returning to our two examples, we can illustrate ongoing strategy evaluation. John's father initiated a second discussion about his son's interests, and then remembering not to push, waited for John to bring the subject up again. Two weeks went by, with no further mention of John's concern. The father reconsidered his plan, and one evening asked John if he was still concerned. The son indicated that he was, but didn't know how to proceed. The father explained to John that he was sensitive to the issue of being pushy. John said he appreciated his father's concern, but that he would not be offended if his father took more initiative. Consequently, the father revised his approach. He would let a week pass without John's initiating a conversation about his future, and then would bring up the subject himself. The following week he asked John if he had done any thinking about the future. John said he had and they had a good discussion. During the following weeks, John initiated several discussions and his plans began to take shape.

In the instance of Helen and Mrs. Gordon, Helen continued her periodic shopping contacts, accepted presents as agreed, and observed that Mrs. Gordon was a much more active and happy person. Her strategy apparently paid off, and there was no need to revise it.

ADDITIONAL EXAMPLES

To reinforce and increase your understanding of the five-step strategy development procedure, we provide additional examples. Each example represents a different situation.

Family Problems

Marge was a second-year student attending community college. She had moved from her parents' home into an apartment during her first year, primarily because she and her father had had many conflicts about values and behavior. Marge would not abide by her father's rules, and they argued constantly. All concerned viewed the apartment as a more satisfactory living arrangement. Marge worked part-time, but still received some financial assistance from her parents. Recently her father had accused her of smoking pot and engaging in promiscuous sexual behavior. He refused to give her further financial assistance, and banned her from the family home. Unhappy about her family relationships and concerned over the problem of financing college, she turned to her Uncle Bob for help. Initially she asked him to "talk to her father and get him to be reasonable."

Bob wanted to help, but what could he do, and how? He employed the five-step procedure and his thinking went something like this:

What are her desired outcomes?: After talking with Marge for awhile, there seem to be three outcomes involved: Marge wants to *(a)* clarify her own feelings about the situation; *(b)* reestablish communication with her parents; and *(c)* reestablish the former, or locate a new, source of financial assistance.

What tools are appropriate? There are several tools I can use to help Marge achieve each of the three outcomes:

1 Clarification—I can listen to her, provide some feedback, and reinforce her working to establish a more satisfactory relationship with her father.

2 Facilitating communication—I can help her plan how she will talk with her father, and role play the situation with her. I can meet with Marge and her father to facilitate their communication by attempting to clarify and check perceptions.

3 Financial information—I can refer her to the community college financial aid office for information about loans and scholarships.

Identify Constraints:

1 Authority—I have none, so it's not a constraint on what I do.

2 Confidentiality—It's likely to be an issue. Her father's accusations may be correct and if she reveals that to me I would feel that I couldn't pass the information on to her father. Marge and I need to get clear on that issue. There may be limits on what I will do.

3 Commitment—I want to help Marge, but I don't want to get into a time-consuming unpleasant situation with in-laws. This definitely constrains what I will do.

4 Psychological closeness—It's not an issue. I'm not that closely involved with either Marge or her parents.

5 Dependency—It might be an issue, but I doubt it. Marge really wants to be on her own.

Applying his conclusions regarding constraints to his tentative strategy, Bob decided that the tentative strategy seemed appropriate. He would, however, clarify the confidentiality matter and indicate that he would restrict his meetings with Marge's parents to one or two.

Begin and evaluate: Bob met with his niece to begin clarifying her feelings about the situation. He anticipated meeting with her parents as well, but at the conclusion of a couple of talks, Marge indicated that she thought that she could handle that by herself. Bob supported that decision, indicated he would be available if she needed him, and encouraged her to continue with her own plan. Thus he was able to terminate his strategy before completing it, or so it seemed. Two weeks had passed when he received a phone call from Marge. She had approached her parents but the conversation was short. Conflicts arose immediately and they parted angrily. Marge asked if Bob was still willing to meet with her and her parents. She hoped he could keep the lid on everyone's emotions. Bob agreed to meet if her parents bought the plan. They did, and a useful meeting was held. Not all the problems were resolved, but he helped get the issues out in the open and to have both Marge and her parents acknowledge that they existed and that they all wanted to resolve them.

Helping A Group

Consider a situation involving a group of people. Alice is in charge of the publication and printing division in a fairly large municipal project. She and other division heads have been asked to meet with top management to devise more effective personnel procedures. Alice has held a variety of positions in the project and thus knows more about the various aspects of the operation than do most of her colleagues. In some respects, she is much better informed regarding operational details than the manager who is chairing the meeting. She observes during the first hour that people are not leveling with the manager about some of their real concerns, and he apparently can't gain enough of the group's confidence to permit honest and candid disclosures. In short she observes that the group is not clear as to its purposes, is wandering aimlessly, and lacks confidence in its nominal leader. She would like to be helpful, and thinks of several things which she might do to aid the group. Before moving blindly into a helping situation, however, she develops a strategy. Her thoughts are as follows:

> At least three outcomes seem important: *(a)* clarifying the group's purpose, *(b)* establishing a more effective procedure, and *(c)* building some confidence in the leader. Given my experience and background, I could probably point out examples of personnel problems. I could also volunteer to work up more examples after interviewing several employees. Regarding the procedures and leadership outcomes, I could suggest that we debrief what has taken place so far, and then develop a more purposeful procedure.

Alice then considered possible constraints:

1 Authority—I don't have it, but it exists. I would need to get permission to change our meeting procedures. I think the manager would see most suggestions or observations about our efforts so far as threatening to his authority.

2 Confidentiality—If I were to give specific examples of some of the personnel issues and problems, I would in a sense break some employee confidences. This is a real constraint to becoming specific about the issues.

3 Commitment—I doubt whether the manager can really pull off his assignment, and I'm not interested in taking on any responsibility besides attending these meetings. I already have plenty to do. No real commitment to helping this group beyond our meetings.

4 Psychological closeness—Not an issue. I'm very objective about the situation.

5 Dependency—Not an issue.

"Given all that," she asked herself, "what can I do to be helpful?" She decided on the following strategy:

I will make an effort to establish more effective procedures and initiate providing more pertinent information. I can model a more open, trusting, task-oriented role. I can also reinforce the manager when he demonstrates effective leadership behavior. I may be able to provide examples of critical issues in terms which are general enough to avoid breaking the confidence of an employee.

She began to implement her strategy and observed that soon others were following her lead. The manager also appeared more relaxed and comfortable with the group, thus paving the way for a more productive effort. Alice had been helpful, and left the meeting without unwanted additional responsibilities.

Strategies aren't always that simple nor do they always work out as well as those described so far. Even though one basic purpose of having strategies is to maintain some control over one's involvement as a helper, even with good helping strategies things can still get out of hand. It's at that point that revisions in one's strategy need to be made.

Hidden Expectations

Consider as a final illustration a situation in which a helper suddenly finds herself with an unwanted obligation. Our heroine, call her Jane, had no children of her own, and from time to time had assisted children of others. Bonnie, a senior in high school, was one such person. Jane had employed Bonnie on a part-time basis to do house cleaning and had talked with Bonnie for the past two years about her college plans. Bonnie's great desire was to go away to school and she had applied to several colleges. As the time went by and suspense regarding admission heightened, Jane became increasingly emotionally involved in the issue.

The climax came in February, and involved both good and bad news. The good news was that Bonnie had been admitted; the bad was no scholarship award. Bonnie had to have financial assistance in order to attend college away from home.

Bonnie told the news to Jane, who was disappointed. She offered to talk through the situation with Bonnie and try to help develop alternatives. Jane's helping strategy was to include supportive listening, providing information and contributing whatever ideas she could. In addition, she offered to contact several friends of hers at the university regarding part-time jobs and possible low-cost housing.

Within a short period of time an offer for a part-time job came through, as did an opportunity for a good but inexpensive room. With some skimping here and there, and by taking out a small loan for the second semester, it seemed that Bonnie could complete the year in college. The only hitch was that in order to obtain the housing, Bonnie had to have a responsible adult cosign a nine months' lease. Her parents had separated years ago and the father had not been heard from since. Her mother was supporting four children on a low salary, and Bonnie would simply not ask her to become involved in her financial problems.

After carefully thinking through the various implications as well as her own motives, Jane offered to cosign the lease, and in September Bonnie left for college, happy and with great expectations. A nice example of an effective helping strategy?

Well, almost. About the first of December, Jane had a phone call from Bonnie. College wasn't at all as she had hoped. Bonnie found her life difficult, unfriendly, and generally disappointing. In short, she had withdrawn from school and was returning home, hoping to find a job. She also asked what she should do about the room lease. She had no funds, and the landlord would probably be sending Jane the bill until it was rerented, which might not be for several months. It seems that the room was very small and not such a bargain after all. There was no question that Jane was responsible for the remainder of the lease.

Now there are a number of solutions to Jane's problem—and some of us would see it as less of a trauma than others. At the least, however, it is an inconvenience for Jane, and probably a cause of personal disappointment. What was wrong with the helping strategy, if anything? Should Jane have cosigned the lease? Why? You will have additional opportunities to work with strategies in Chapter 9.

SUMMARY

This chapter has been concerned with developing helping strategies, which are plans for using helping tools. A five-step procedure for developing strategies has been discussed and illustrated. The steps are aimed at (1) identifying desired outcomes of helping, (2) selecting appropriate tools for a tentative strategy, (3) modifying the tentative strategy in light of consideration of the underlying relationship, (4) implementing the help, and (5) evaluating and modifying the strategy as help is offered.

Let's be realistic. There are many times when it isn't necessary to use the strategy model. It may be enough to simply consider the five points before deciding what to do. The primary difficulties occur when constraints are not identified. Therefore, whether our helping is for a short time or involves a complex set of procedures, prior consideration of strategy helps to avoid getting into situations illustrated by thoughts such as: "I wish she hadn't told me that," or "I really don't want all of this unloaded on me," or "I don't have the time or interest to deal with this," or "I can't meet their unrealistic expectations and I wish I had said so to begin with."

It is usually wise, in other words, to have a plan and establish some limits before initiating a helping relationship.

EXERCISES

To get more practice in developing helping strategies, follow the procedure described below:

1   In your journal, record problems that acquaintances describe to you.

2   For each problem description, outline a helping strategy as described on pages 152–158.

3   To get feedback on your strategies, review your plan with someone else and specifically discuss the following:

—Does the plan seem realistic?
—Do you have the skills necessary to carry out the plan?

As a result of this exercise, do you feel more confident in developing helping strategies? If not, how could you gain more confidence?

Nine | Practicing Strategies

An interesting way to conclude our helping project would be to discuss illustrative situations and compare alternative helping strategies. But that's not possible because you are there and we are wherever we are. What we can do is make it possible for you to compare your strategies with ours. We will describe several situations in which helping appears appropriate. Following each situation, space is provided for you to work out and describe your strategy—what you would do to be helpful in the situation. Then one of us has noted what we would do, and the reasons for doing it, and the other of us comments on the strategy. If there are differences, as there will be, it doesn't mean that we are right and you are wrong, or vice versa. There are often many strategies which would be effective in a given situation. They will reflect the personality of the helper, your particular skills, and the nature of the underlying relationship with the person being helped. The point of making these comparisons is to illustrate that there can be several strategies which are appropriate for a given situation. There is no single perfect strategy.

To make the comparisons more useful, we're suggesting two ground rules. First use the five steps described in Chapter 8. Don't write any more than is necessary to outline your helping plan, but do use the general format of the five steps. We'll do the same. Second, assume that you are you, rather than a helper in a fictitious role, even if the person or persons you're helping *are* fictitious. By so doing, you can highlight the impact of your own personality, conditions, and relationships on helping strategies. Again, we will do the same. In each of the following examples, Ripley describes the strategy and Loughary is the commentor.

RETIREMENT

Situation

Imagine that a couple you know has been retired for about a year. It might be your parents, other relatives, or friends. Assume that you know them well and are interested in their well-being. You are in the midst of having coffee with them, and notice that they seem to be irritating one another. The bickering quickly develops into what could be a full-blown argument. The issue seems trivial to you. As you prepare to leave, the couple seem to realize that they have been preoccupied with their private spat, apologize for their behavior, and urge you to stay. You do.

"We do that a lot lately," comments the husband. "Argue over insignificant events, I mean. It seems to have started shortly after I retired."

"Not at first," his wife corrects. "At first it was wonderful having so much time together, but within a short while we just seemed to get on one another's nerves more and more."

"Any idea why?" you ask.

"Too much time and nothing to do," answers the husband.

"Maybe for you, but not for me," his wife suggests. "I've got the same things to do now as before you retired. My life hasn't really changed—except that you're home all day."

"I suppose you're right," he agrees. "But this retirement isn't what it's supposed to be. It's downright boring a lot of the time."

"Well, that's your doing, not mine," his wife concludes.

Seeing a possible opportunity to be helpful, and believing that this couple could gain more satisfaction from their retirement, you suggest:

"Maybe only one of you retired, and the other is still working, so to speak."

"That may be right," she agrees, "but how can I retire? I quit my job ten years ago, the kids left long ago, and I've got a regular pattern to my life. It's he that needs to change."

"If you look at it as 'his' retirement, then that's right," you acknowledge, "but what if you both view his retirement as an opportunity for both of you to change your life styles as individuals and as a couple?"

They appear interested in your suggestion. "Do you mind talking about this some more?" she asks, and he nods in agreement.

Reader, how would you proceed? What would you do to provide help? Take a moment to think about the couple's problem and follow the steps listed below, noting how you would:

1 *Translate the problem into outcomes*

2 *Choose tools*

3 *Consider constraints*

4 *Begin*

5 *Evaluate*

Fill in the blank spaces before continuing to read. We've put our minds to the same problem, and share our ideas about it below. Compare your strategy with ours.

Helping Strategy: Our Report

1 *Translate the problem* The issue here is a little trickier than most because being able to state a desired outcome *is* the outcome. Read that sentence again. Here is a couple that is trying to decide what to do with this next phase of their lives.

2 *Choose tools* As a helper, I want to assist them in making an effective decision. Decision-making tools, communication tools, resource tools, and feedback tools will all be useful in this effort.

3 *Consider constraints* I see no issue with authority or confidentiality; these are favorite relatives, and I am willing and able to commit time. The only difficulty might be psychological closeness since I think I tend to put a halo around this couple. I must watch my objectivity.

4 *Begin* Since I know they are willing readers and learners, I suggest they read *Dynamic Retirement,* and that we discuss it the following week. My intention is that we review those worksheets in the book that refer to values and goals, and then to do more systematic decision making. I will give feedback when appropriate.

5 *Evaluate* I am surprised to find a week later that they have followed many of the suggestions in the book and even sought out a retirement counselor at the senior citizen's center to assist them. I found I was out of a job!

Comment

The couple I thought of in this situation would probably not have taken as readily to completing worksheets as Ripley's couple did. I would probably have offered to model this activity by doing a worksheet with them and then discussing it. I like the point about psychological closeness. It would be easy to overwhelm the couple with help; in other words, to take over. Probably the most difficult aspect of this situation is helping the couple be specific about goals. For the most part, they have let circumstances (e.g., job, family) define goals for them. Now, for the husband at least, those circumstances no longer exist. It's difficult to become self-directive at this point in one's life span. Attention might be given to skills for expressing feelings. If the couple in their new circumstances are experiencing different feelings than before retirement, then bringing this up, acknowledging its importance, and modeling the expression of feeling without making accusations could be appropriate. We don't know from the information presented if it is an issue.

One of the best aspects of Ripley's strategy is that she keeps it simple. Her intention, as a helper, is realistic and reasonable in scope. She focuses on helping the couple clarify the changes in their relationship brought on by retirement and in formulating goals. She carefully avoids taking on responsibility for guiding their retirement.

SPENDING

Situation

Now, assume you are talking with a friend of yours, a woman about thirty years old, married, mother of two children, and employed as a salesperson in a popular clothing store. You might be her supervisor or a good friend. Whatever the relationship, authority is there but not a problem; she knows you care about her. Over the several years you have known this person, you have been aware of her tendency to make what seem to be many major purchases—new furniture, appliances, clothes, and even automobiles.

Your present conversation turns to the rising cost of living. With a sigh, she says:

"That's part of the problem, but not all of it."

"The problem?" you reflect.

"Yes, everything costs more, but Bill and I really do seem to overspend. I'm ashamed to admit it, but we had two credit cards canceled last month, and I don't think we can pay all of our bills this month."

"That's not good."

"Worse. The bank called Bill's employer this week. We're a car payment behind. I think we must be spendaholics!"

"That's upsetting. What have you tried as a cure?" you ask.

"We've talked about it a lot. But we never get out of debt. We agree to cut down spending, but then one of us will go out and buy something. I'm really getting concerned. Besides the money problem, our relationship is being affected. About all we do is argue about financial problems. I really wish someone could help find an answer. I'm ready to do anything!"

Reader, how would you respond? Why? Again, try your ideas as you play the helper role before reading ours.

1 *Translate the problem into outcomes*

2 *Choose tools*

3 *Consider constraints*

4 *Begin*

5 *Evaluate*

Helping Strategy: Our Report

1 *Translate the problem* In this example, I will assume that I am this woman's supervisor and also a friend. I assume that the following two desired outcomes would emerge as goals:
a To learn more effective money-management skills.
b To increase her ability to talk effectively with spouse about financial concerns.

2 *Choose tools* Since I've known Joan, finances and over-spending have always been a concern. She and her spouse have developed a pattern that is very well established by this time. I suspect that she does not understand her attitudes and values regarding money and spending, and that this is part of the problem. I think that she would probably want to change some of those values once they were acknowledged. Consequently, I would use various communication skills (particularly probing) to help clarify underlying values. I could then model more effective ways of budgeting and actually show her how to make a monthly/yearly budget. I would suggest a contract whereby she and her husband prepare a monthly budget, try to follow it, and then meet with me to debrief her experience. Regarding the arguing, I could model and then role play with Joan effective ways to communicate with her husband.

3 *Consider constraints* As far as constraints, there is no issue with authority and psychological closeness, but I am concerned that Joan's husband would be very "uptight" about my knowing about their family finances. Even though I know I would keep the information confidential, I'm sure he would be most concerned. But the big issue is really one of commitment. To do what I outlined would take a lot of time, and I am not willing to do it. I believe a better alternative would be to refer Joan and her husband to the financial counselor at the company credit union.

4 *Begin* I will choose an appropriate time when I do not feel rushed, to discuss the referral with joan. I know the name of a specific counselor, and I can describe how and when to contact him.

5 *Evaluate* I would follow up with Joan one to two weeks later to show that I am concerned and to see if she could give me feedback on the helpfulness of the person to whom I referred her.

Comment

I agree with the commitment concerns. If Joan's problem with overspending is as serious as suggested, then it will not be solved overnight. As long as you have confidence in the financial counselor, then the referral seems appropriate. In this instance, a blind referral would seem inappropriate. That is, simply suggesting that Joan "go talk with the credit union" would seem a cavalier response to a serious problem. The only suggestion I have is possibly telling Joan what she might expect from the financial counselor such as requests for specific information on income, expenses, and debts. I would suggest that she make lists of such information. In addition to the financial counselor's needing it, the process of writing it down may help Joan clarify her spending habits.

ALONENESS

Situation

A friend of yours who has been divorced about three months telephones you one evening. (If you haven't got a divorced friend, imagine that a married or separated friend becomes divorced.) This friend, whom you haven't talked with for a couple of weeks, indicates that the call is simply to make contact. He or she openly acknowledges the need to begin to revise a life style of being married to one of being single. As the conversation progresses, your friend expresses concern about an inability to cope with aloneness. Eating irregularly, drinking more, and spending large amounts of time watching dull TV are symptomatic. In addition to the feeling that this is an inadequate adjustment to the divorce, your friend is becoming a little scared of what the future holds or, more to the point, doesn't hold. Is aimlessness a natural consequence of divorce which will pass, or is it something more serious? Do you have any suggestions? You believe your friend's claim of not wanting to impose upon you, yet you want to help. What would you do? Could you be of help? In this one, be careful to avoid becoming a marriage counselor or therapist. This isn't a neurotic cry for help, but rather a friend asking for assistance in solving a relatively straightforward problem. What would you do?

1 *Translate the problem into outcomes*

2 *Choose tools*

3 *Consider constraints*

4 *Begin*

5 *Evaluate*

Helping Strategy: Our Report

1 *Translate the problem* After talking with my friend a bit more, we both acknowledged that there are a lot of concerns in her life. We continue to clarify until we come up with an outcome that, stated formally, is:

I want to spend my weekends and evenings in ways I see as productive. In clarifying the desired outcome, a number of communication skills were used, and we have come from a global (I'm lonely) to a more specific, tangible concern (I want my weekends and evenings to be productive).

2 *Choose tools* I could encourage my friend to make a list of alternative ways she could have productive evenings/weekends. Then together we could go through the rest of the decision-making model (estimating resources, risks, and preferences) to select the best alternatives. I would encourage her to make a schedule of activities and share it with me. If it seemed that an initial daily phone contact with me would be an effective external reward to getting started, I would agree to that.

3 *Consider constraints* In this instance I see no constraints. No issue with confidentiality, authority, or psychological closeness; and I am willing to make some commitment of time, although I don't imagine it will be very demanding.

4 *Begin* I will try to start the helping process on an upbeat. Without being "Pollyannish," I can encourage an attitude of growth and new challenges regarding her new life situation, although I can acknowledge that a period of adjustment is understandable.

5 *Evaluate* After the new activities are chosen, I might be able to make more specific suggestions and referrals when she is a week or two into her schedule.

Comment

Two things occur to me. One is the importance of helping your friend select activities which are highly "doable." Sometimes the activities which one would enjoy most are difficult to do. If skiing, for example, is at the top of her list and going to a film has lower priority, selecting the latter may be the best initial choice. The chief concern, in other words, is getting a satisfying new pattern going as quickly as possible. Initially, the specific activity is not as important as having satisfaction. The second comment, and this is obvious, is offering to do an activity with your friend. Depending upon the constraints, which you say are minimal, that may be the most powerful way to help. By doing an activity with her, you can probably add assurance that it will be enjoyable.

KIDS

Situation

The concern in this instance is helping a friend who is upset regarding his poor relationship with a teenage son. Your friend has mentioned his concern to you from time to time, and the issue arises in today's conversation:

> "It's getting to me," he admits. "It gets worse and worse. The only times we talk are when there are problems. Either he's screwing up at school, being inconsiderate at home, or just plain unpleasant. There's never a pleasant moment with that kid, and it just tears me up."
>
> "You've tried talking with him about your concerns?"
>
> "Sure—doesn't work. He says what he does is none of my business."
>
> "Tried the neutral activity bit?"
>
> "I've offered, but he doesn't take me up. Would rather be with his buddies, and I can understand that."
>
> "Whatever, you are more concerned than in the past," you observe.
>
> "Yeah. Worry is one thing, but I'm preoccupied with the problem. It's like I expect him to screw up, and he does. I'm waiting for the other shoe to drop, if you know what I mean."

Here we have a father who has two problems, not just one. His problem, as he sees it, is getting his son to be more responsible and pleasant. His second problem, as revealed if not stated explicitly, is changing his own debilitating feelings about the situation. Probably the obvious way to solve the second problem is to solve the first. That is, if the son will change his behavior to suit the father, then the father won't have anything to worry about, at least in regard to his son. But let's consider the possibility that the boy isn't going to change his behavior, or at least not for awhile. Or, assume that the father's concern for his son on the one hand, and his own debilitating feelings about the son on the other, may require separate solutions. The father, of course, hasn't thought of that. He assumes that the only solution to relieving his anxiety is for his son to shape up. How could you help him redefine the problem?

1 *Translate the problem into outcomes*

2 *Choose tools*

3 *Consider constraints*

4 *Begin*

5 *Evaluate*

Helping Strategy: Our Report

1 *Translate the problem* My friend, after further discussion and using debriefing, realizes that changing his son's behavior and his feelings are two different problems, and he agrees that he will focus on the latter as a concern. His desired outcome, after more thought, is to minimize the effect of the negative feelings generated by his son's behavior.

2 *Choose tools* I describe the process of self-debriefing to my friend and suggest that while it is not a cure-all, it might be a useful means of better understanding what's irritating him. In the interest of collecting information about the problem, I suggest that the father keep a journal of the debriefings. I state that I will be willing to listen to what he's written in the journal to provide an outlet for his feelings.

3 *Consider constraints* There are no constraints involved, and I am willing to commit myself to a half hour a week of listening.

4 *Begin* I suggest we schedule our talks so that it is more likely to occur.

5 *Evaluate* After three weeks, my friend is still mostly complaining about his son's behavior. He continues to confuse his displeasure with the son and his own feelings. I will probably use confrontation to help him separate the two issues.

Comment

A tough problem. It is often difficult to separate a condition from our feelings about the condition. It's a psychological version of an optical illusion. In addition to confronting the father with his continued complaining and focusing on the boy's behavior, I would probably add structure to the journal by suggesting that he use three columns, side by side. Label the first "Boy's Behavior," the second "My Reactions," and the third "Action." I would suggest that he note daily both the behavior and his reaction, thus encouraging him to distinguish between the two. Under the "Action" column, he would record what he did about his reaction, or note what he could do the next time he has a similar reaction. It's a good example of the "you make me angry" myth. You don't make me angry, of course; I make myself angry in response to something I observed you do. Nevertheless, it's a difficult distinction to make because most of us have been led to believe that it's others, not ourselves, who cause our feelings.

MORE KIDS

Situation

Young people are often concerned about the plights of their peers, but are not in a position to provide help beyond listening. They sometimes try to enlist adults in a helping campaign.

Assume you have a teenage daughter, niece, or close friend. She has commented several times during the last few months on her friend Lynn's situation. Lynn is seventeen and the oldest of four children. Her parents expect Lynn to baby-sit when they are not home. Such occasions occur frequently and include nearly all weekend evenings. Consequently, Lynn is not able to participate in social activities with her friends. She has asked her parents to be more considerate, but they indicate that their expectations regarding the baby-sitting are reasonable; it's her means of contributing to the family. According to your daughter (or niece or friend), Lynn is seriously thinking about leaving home. She thinks she can get a part-time job and knows of a room she can share. Your daughter asks if you can help. She believes that Lynn's parents are unrealistic in comparison with what other parents expect of young people, and that it would not take much giving-in on their part to satisfy Lynn. You know Lynn, and see her as a responsible, pleasant, and reasonable young person. You've never met her parents. How would you respond to this request for help?

1 *Translate the problem into outcomes*

2 *Choose tools*

3 *Consider constraints*

4 *Begin*

5 *Evaluate*

Helping Strategy: Our Report

1 *Translate the problem* In clarifying the issue with Lynn, I am careful not to make value judgments about her decision to move out. After more discussion, Lynn says she really does not want to move out, but she believes that is the only way to get free time to spend with her friends. She states her real desire is to go "half-way" with her folks:— I would like to have every other Saturday and one weekend night per week free to go out.

2 *Choose tools* Now we have a negotiation problem. Lynn and I discuss various ways to approach her folks. Without evaluating the alternatives, we come up with this list:

a I could talk with her parents.

b A favorite teacher could be asked to talk with her parents.

c Lynn could talk with her parents.

d Lynn could write her proposal to her folks and follow it up with a discussion.

We discuss these alternatives and their advantages and disadvantages and also the risks involved. Each alternative would necessitate different helping tools and strategy; I am using decision-making tools with Lynn.

3 *Consider constraints* The only constraint is commitment. I do not want to get heavily involved in a family dispute. In discussing this with Lynn, we agree to eliminate the alternative of my talking with her parents. Lynn decides she wants to approach her parents directly. At my suggestion, we agree to role play the scene with her parents.

4 *Begin* Lynn says she wants to think about what she wants to say, and we agree to get together the next day for practice. At that time my niece and I play her parents and we role play and offer feedback.

5 *Evaluate* I ask Lynn to report back after she talks with her parents, and she excitedly called the next day with a positive report.

Comment

This is a good example of helping without intervening in an actual situation or relationship. The tendency of many people would be to focus on what seems to be the crux of the problem, the parents' attitude. The likelihood of a stranger making much difference via a direct intervention would appear very low. It makes much more sense to concentrate on helping the young woman to deal with the issue by herself. There is a related concern, however, and that is the parents' possible reactions to knowing that their daughter consulted an outsider regarding a family problem. Would they be resentful or defensive and thus even less likely to negotiate a new arrangement? It would probably be well to discuss this with Lynn, and let her decide whether or not to tell her parents about your discussions. The strategy also illustrates an effective use of role playing. Lynn enters the negotiation session with her parents both with purpose and "experience." The role playing enabled her to "experience" many of the feelings, questions, and arguments which were present in the actual discussion. She had, in other words, reduced the uncertainty about this difficult and important meeting.

QUICKIES

Finally, let's compare notes on some quickies, some specific kinds of problems which are fairly common. In the incidences that follow, we want to focus on identifying alternative goals and helping behavior. The purpose, in other words, is to list as many kinds of assistance you could provide rather than outlining a particular helping strategy. Our lists of alternatives follow the spaces for your lists.

Job Change

You have a friend who's been a school teacher for ten years. He says he's fed up. He wants to do something more challenging where he'll have a chance to be rewarded on the basis of what he produces. He wants to feel that he is being creative and more in charge of his destiny. Besides reading the classified ads in the newspaper, he has no idea of how to make a change. How could you help?

YOUR ALTERNATIVES

OUR LIST

1   Encourage him to describe more specifically what he wants from a job.

2   Refer him to a college career-planning and placement office.

3 Encourage investigating vocational aptitude testing through the employment service.

4 Refer him to books on career planning (see Chapter 10).

5 Have him list all of his skills.

6 Suggest examining the leisure aspect of his life as a source of challenge.

Mobility

You've known Mary for nearly a year. She and her family will be moving to a different city next week. Mary has moved thirteen times in as many years of married life. Every time she begins to get settled-in and know a few people, her husband is transferred. She knows that two alternative solutions are a change in job for her husband and divorce. Short of these, she would like some help in devising ways to cope with her nomadic life style, which does have certain attractive aspects such as travel and change. What could you suggest.

YOUR ALTERNATIVES

OUR LIST

1 Encourage her to write you once a week describing adjustment experiences.

2 Encourage her to keep a journal describing her nomadic life style.

3 Consider joining a club which has chapters in many cities.

4 Subscribe by mail to the new city's newspapers.

5 Ask friends for possible contacts in the new city.

6 Find a newcomer's group.

7 Start a newcomer's group.

Skills Needed

A friend whose children are grown became involved in volunteer activities as a way of adding meaning to her life. She has no employment experiences. After serving in a clerical position in the volunteer's club, she became a program coordinator for two successive terms in that organization. Much to her surprise, she was nominated for vice president of the club, a position which normally leads to the presidency. Knowing that she had a year to observe and gain experience as vice president, she agreed to run, and won. A week following the election, the president resigned and your friend was elevated to head of the organization. Her immediate reaction was apprehension. She had never been an officer or even an active member of a club until now. She thought of resigning, but realized that someone must be president. How could she quickly prepare to carry out at least the basic responsibilities of the presidency? She asks you for suggestions.

YOUR ALTERNATIVES

OUR LIST

1   Help her outline basic tasks and responsibility.

2   Encourage her to go to city council meetings to observe the chairperson.

3   Encourage her to role play in front of the mirror.

4   Model appropriate behavior to her.

5   Encourage her to write down everything she's going to do at the meeting.

6   Encourage her to contact other female presidents of organizations and discuss how to assume her responsibility.

7   Suggest borrowing a "how to run a meeting" book from the library.

8   Offer to provide feedback following meetings.

Grief

A coworker experienced the death of a close family member about three months ago. Following the initial grief, he or she began to recover and return to previous patterns of activities and interests. Yesterday you saw your friend staring out of the window, seemingly very unhappy. When you asked if anything was wrong, your friend told you that in the last week life has been a preoccupation with sad thoughts, restless nights, and mounting preoccupation with death. Your coworker thought that getting a good start on new interests and activities would make the difference. But the pattern seems impossible to change. Your coworker asked if you could help.

YOUR ALTERNATIVES

OUR LIST

1 Buy them the book *How to Survive the Loss of a Love* which outlines the process of grief and gives helpful suggestions.

2 Suggest you start a new activity together.

3 Encourage him or her to talk with you about feelings of loss, sadness.

4 Offer to listen in the future if grief persists or returns.

5 Suggest scheduling enjoyable activities and making commitments to do them.

6 Join a widow or widower's group.

Investments

A friend of some long-standing greets you with a large smile. When you inquire why, she happily reveals recent news of an unexpected inheritance. "Never mind the complicated explanation," she said, "just believe that I am to get nearly $50,000."

Then her smile changed to a concerned frown as she noted that she hasn't the slightest notion, beyong putting the money in savings, of what to do with her wealth. She is an intelligent person who has a moderate income, so this could be investment money. "What about stocks, bonds, real estate, or whatever?" she asked. "Where can I get some good advice?"

Assuming that the Brooklyn Bridge is not for sale, what would you suggest?

YOUR ALTERNATIVES

1 Buy her a copy of *Joy of Money or New Money Dynamics.*

2 Encourage her to take a class at the local community college on investing.

3 Encourage her to interview three professionals in each area she is considering investing (stockbrokers, real estate brokers) before selecting one to work with.

4 Interview someone who teaches investment courses.

5 Interview the manager of a credit union.

6 Subscribe to the *Wall Street Journal.*

7 Begin reading financial columns in newspapers and magazines.

If you are interested in learning more about helping strategies, you may find the books listed below helpful.

REFERENCES

Benjamin, Alfred: *The Helping Interview,* 2d ed., Boston: Houghton Mifflin, 1974.

Brammer, L.: *The Helping Relationship: Process and Skills,* 2d ed., Englewood Cliffs, N.J.: Prentice-Hall, 1979.

Carkhuff, R. R.: *Helping and Human Relations, vol. I: Selection and Training.* New York: Holt, 1969a.

Carkhuff, R. R.: *Helping and Human Relations, vol. II: Practice and Research.* New York: Holt, 1969b.

Danish, Steven and Allen Haver: *Helping Skills: A Basic Training Program.* New York: Human Sciences Press, 1976.

Egan, G.: *The Skilled Helper: A Model for Systematic Helping and Interpersonal Relating.* Monterey, California: Brooks/Cole, 1975.

Ivey, A.: *Microcounseling: Innovations in Interview Training.* Springfield, Ill.: Thomas Publishing, 1971.

Johnson, D. W.: *Reaching Out: Interpersonal Effectiveness and Self-Actualization.* Englewood Cliffs, N.J.: Prentice-Hall, 1972.

We noted in the beginning that helping is a process. It involves a problem, a purpose, a beginning, helping tools, strategies, and an end or outcome. The process stops and then you begin again with different people, different circumstances. Change is what is certain, and a good part of life is helping to make changes satisfying for others as well as oneself.

This book itself was intended to be a helping process, and it is now ending. We hope the outcomes have been to make you more understanding of the nature of helping and more effective at doing it. As with many human activities, satisfaction is a function of both one's ability to perform and an appreciation of the subtleties involved in what one is doing. It's not just what we do, but how well we think about what we do that makes the difference.

Ten | Information Resources

One of the most important helping resources available is information. Ignorance can be a terrible handicap when we are attempting to make decisions and plans. There are several topics about which many people need information. For those we have listed several basic information resources which should be useful to helpers and those who seek help. The sources of information listed in this section are available in public, school, or college libraries, or can be obtained by writing to the sources indicated. References have been organized according to the following six categories:

1 Educational Opportunities and Plans

2 Finances

3 Leisure

4 Married, Single, In Between

5 Occupational Plans and Opportunities

6 Parenting

7 Retirement

There is a great deal of factual and straightforward "where to go for a specific service" information available about some of the categories. In contrast, while there is an increasing amount of information available regarding marriage and family problems, most of it is of a "self-help" variety. Given the amount of human grief generated from problems involved in marriage and family relationships and the often expressed need for help with them, we have included books and pamphlets which we believe can be helpful.

Remember that only a very small sampling of information resources is presented. Those presented have been found to be helpful, and can form the beginning of a set of information resources. Many of the books described are relatively inexpensive paperbacks. Books which are library references are indicated by an asterisk (*).

EDUCATIONAL OPPORTUNITIES AND PLANS

Four-Year Colleges and Universities
GENERAL INFORMATION

The College Blue Book: 10 vols., New York: CCM Information Corporation, latest edition.
This is probably the most comprehensive and detailed educational directory available. The content of each volume is summarized below. The summaries are excerpted from Volume 4.

Volume 1: *Guide and Index to College Blue Book*
The section, "How to Use the College Blue Book," includes the new Student Form for College Selection, as well as guidelines for selecting a college and planning for it. There are complete instructions on how-to-use for each volume in this section.

The section, "Special Lists of Colleges," includes lists of colleges accepting "C" students; predominantly black colleges; women's colleges; men's colleges; two-year colleges; and colleges offering ROTC.

Analytical Index to all volumes of CBB, in alphabetical order.

Volume 2: *U.S. Colleges: Tabular Data*
Over 3,400 U.S. colleges are listed alphabetically by state, in an easy-to-read, two-color tabular format. Information about entrance requirements, costs, accreditation, enrollment figures, faculty, location, year founded, ROTC, and the names of the chief administrative officer and registrar are given for each school. Each of the 3,400 institutions has a unique number which ties it to the narrative description given in Volume 3.

Volume 3: *U.S. Colleges: Narrative Descriptions*
Each of the 3,400 colleges listed in Volume 2 is fully described in Volume 3. Exact procedures are given for filing admission applications, and campus facilities are discussed.

Volume 4: *Degrees Offered, by Subject*
Over 2,100 subject areas for which degrees are granted by one or more institutions of higher education are listed in alphabetical order. Colleges offering degrees in each subject are listed in state order.

Volume 5: *Degrees Offered, by College*
Each of the more than 3,400 colleges listed in Volumes 2 and 3 appears in

Volume 5, in alphabetical order by state. Under the name of each college appears a list of the subject areas for which they offer degrees.

Volume 6: *College Atlas*
This volume describes the geographical location of each of the schools listed in Volumes 2 and 3. Airline routes, bus and train schedules, as well as highway information, are given for each town. In addition, a full-page map of each state identifies the location of all colleges within the state.

Volume 7: *Specialized Educational Programs*
This volume offers information about many educational opportunities available in the United States and abroad. Associated institutions of higher education are listed and described; complete information on church-related colleges and universities is given; general information regarding accredited schools and courses offered through the National Home Study Council is given. Correspondence courses offered by institutions that are affiliated with the National University Extension Association are listed.

In a separate section called "Study Abroad," there is complete information about enrollment, curricula, and tuition for most of the major universities abroad.

Volume 8: *Professions, Careers, and Accreditation*
The first section of this volume, "Choosing a Career," defines and identifies professions and careers likely to be of greatest interest to *College Blue Book* users. Accreditation associations are listed, together with the schools that are accredited by each organization. In addition, professional and educational associations related to the professions listed earlier in the volume are listed and described.

Volume 9: *Scholarships, Fellowships, and Grants*
This volume lists over $1 million in available scholarships, together with information about when and how to apply and who is eligible.

Volume 10: *Secondary Schools in the U.S.*
Over 30,000 junior and senior high schools in the United States are listed with information about type of school and accreditation. In addition, separate lists of parochial and private schools are given.

The College Handbook, New York: College Entrance Examination Board, current edition.
Describes each of the colleges which are affiliated with College Entrance Examination Board. Written for the potential student who has questions in mind.

COLLEGE ADMISSIONS TESTING

American College Testing Program
College Entrance Examination Board

Many colleges require students to take the examinations of one of these organizations as part of their admission procedure. The tests are given several times each year on specified dates. School counselors have the testing schedule and application materials for both programs.

SELECTION SERVICES

Several college admission services are available for students who may have some difficulty gaining college admission and who wish to have their credentials considered by a number of accredited colleges. Two such services are:

The College Admission Service
610 Church Street
Evanston, Illinois 60201
College Admission Center
41 East 65th Street
New York, New York 10021

Two-Year Colleges and Schools

*Campbell, Gordon: *Community College in Canada.* Toronto/New York/ London: Ryerson Press, latest edition.

Brief descriptions of Canadian community colleges listed by province. Includes academic, financial, and admission information.

*Cass, James, and Max Bernbaum: *Comparative Guide to Two-Year Colleges and Four-Year Specialized Schools and Programs.* New York: Harper & Row, latest edition.

Brief listing of many community colleges. Special value is its emphasis on colleges offering programs in the performing arts including art, dance, music, theater, radio, TV, and film.

*Gleazer, Edmond J., ed.: *American Junior Colleges,* 8th ed., Washington: American Council on Education.

Sponsored by the American Council on Education and the American Association of Junior Colleges, this volume describes all two-year institutions accredited by nationally recognized accrediting agencies. Covers all states and territories and lists public and private institutions separately. There is also a listing of two-year institutions according to the programs offered in various occupational fields.

Occupational Education

*Miller, A. E., and B. I. Brown: *National Directory of Schools and Vocations.* No. Springfield, Pa.: State School Publications, latest edition.

Lists colleges according to occupation programs from "accountant to x-ray clerk." An initial reference, little descriptive information.

*Russell, Max W., ed. *The Blue Book of Occupational Education*, New York: CCM Information Corp., latest edition.

Presents information on nearly 12,000 occupational schools in the United States. Describes schools and indexes by programs of instruction offered from accounting to zinc platemaking. The main headings from the table of contents suggest the scope of the book. These are:

Occupational Schools of the United States

Curricula and Programs of Instruction

Accredited Business Schools

Two-Year Institutions of the United States

Accredited Home Study Schools

Schools Offering Two-Year Library Technology Programs

Accredited Medical and Dental Technological Schools of the United States

Nursing Schools of the United States

Schools Approved for Veteran's Training

Apprenticeship Training

United States Occupational Training Programs

Guide to Nation's Job Openings

Financial Aid

Sources of Additional Information

FINANCES

Callenbach, Ernest: *Living Poor With Style.* New York: Bantam, 1972.

For those who want advice on saving money, *Living Poor With Style* is a must. There are a multitude of suggestions regarding expenditures for food, shelter, transportation, furnishings, clothing, medical services, recreation, education and training, and raising children. This advice is laced with comments about governmental policy and social issues. There is a definite basis: it is "in" to be poor and against the mainstream culture. Aware of this, readers can objectively read the ideas and useful hints and judge whether they can use them in their own life style.

Crook De Camp, Catherine: *The Money Tree.* New York: New American Library, 1972.

This book is useful for those who need general information in many financial areas. After reading the book, one inexperienced in money matters should feel more confident.

The book begins with an elementary discussion of assets and liabilities and suggestions for developing a spending plan. Comparative government data on family spending are given. Methods for the art and discipline of record keeping are discussed, and illustrative forms are displayed in the appendix.

Helpful chapters are included on credit buying; building or buying/renting a home; buying a car; and financing a car. In each of these chapters specific information is given regarding who to see, what to look for, and what to compare. Other chapters are included on shopping skills and common fraudulent business practices.

The author also deals with the issues of saving, stocks, and Social Security. The appendix includes a good bibliography.

Ferguson, Marilyn and Mike: *Champagne Living on a Beer Budget.* New York: Berkley, 1973.

The usual topics on consuming or spending wisely in the areas of food, housing, furnishings, clothing, transportation, babies, medicine, gift-giving, recreation, travel. Government benefits are treated. Other topics, not usually treated in similar books, include "how-to" information for saving on telephone rates, stating consumer complaints, investing money, renting almost anything, and planning efficiently.

The writing style of this book makes it particularly interesting and useful. Each chapter includes anecdotes and specific suggestions.

Halcomb, Ruth: *Money and the Working Ms.* Chatsworth, Calif.: Books for Better Living, 1974.

This book is designed to assist the single working woman to do effective financial planning. The author, a single working mother, states that the book's purpose is "to help you initiate a total program for wise spending and saving."

After describing case studies of ineffective women spenders, the author urges the reader to make a master plan complete with goals and a careful study of one's assets and liabilities. The next step is to develop a workable budget. The items of most budgets—food, shelter, furnishings, clothes, entertainment, transportation—are specifically discussed in subsequent chapters, and guidelines are presented for determining the priorities within.

Other financial concerns such as dealing with emergencies and taxes are also discussed. A special chapter discusses economic and psychological problems in raising children alone. The book concludes with a brief discussion of investment possibilities for the single woman.

The Mother Earth News Almanac. New York: Bantam, 1973.

All those interested in a book chock-full of ideas and helpful hints from A to Z will enjoy *The Mother Earth News Almanac.* This 361-page almanac has literally thousands of practical suggestions and "how-to" information. These include ideas which are:

Practical (how to make a compost)

Fun (building a kite)

Old-timey (folk medicine)

Designed for those wanting to get "back to the land" (tips on raising animals)

Helpful hints for improving city and suburban life (how to grow a sprout garden in a closet)

Futuristic (using solar energy for heating homes)

A number of the ideas encountered can save the reader money. A good book for a rainy afternoon, and one you will use as a ready reference thereafter.

Nelson, Paula. *The Joy of Money.* New York: Bantam, 1975.

A well-done book for today's woman—single, divorced, or married. In the seventeen chapters the author overcomes the reader's potential timidity regarding moneymaking to giving some sound advice and making it sound like fun to attain financial freedom. She takes one through the process of goal setting, getting out of debt, choosing your financial professionals, and charting various investment options. Three chapters of the book are devoted to starting your own business.

Poriss, Martin: *How to Live Cheap But Good.* New York: Dell, 1971.   ...,

This book is primarily geared to the apartment dweller and college student but because of the variety and clarity of money-saving hints it is recommended for others as well. The six chapters include the following:

Home Is Where You Find it
Includes hints on how to find and select the best living unit for you.
Deals with signing a lease.
Has apartment hunter's checklist.
A Moving Experience
Includes a step-by-step procedure for moving your possessions.
Shoveling Out, Fixing Up, and Furnishing
Specific advice on cleaning and fixing one's home and furnishings.

Thought for Food

Information ranges from what kind of equipment should be in the kitchen to how one should buy fruits and vegetables and cooking methods and techniques.

Home Repairs for the Poet

Step-by-step procedures for repairing plumbing, electrical fixtures, doors, windows, and radiators.

Getting Your Money's Worth

Includes ideas for saving on clothes, health care, and utility bills as well as how to be an effective consumer.

Porter, Sylvia: *The Money Book.* New York: Avon, 1975.

If you only buy one book on money management, this is the one to buy!

Scaduto, Anthony. *Getting the Most for Your Money.* New York: Paperback Library, 1970.

A real gem for general consumer information such as skills for wise shopping and charts showing which months different items (e.g., appliances, clothing, cars, etc.) are most likely to be on sale. The book deals in depth with major spending items. Chapters are included on:

Buying food

Buying clothes

Household appliance purchases

Buying and maintaining a car

Recreational spending

Financing college educations

Buying property and life insurance

Medical expenses

Each chapter provides specific facts, information, or shopping hints for making the most of your dollar.(For example, the chapter on buying food provides general food-buying hints and specific buying tips for meat, dairy products, baked goods, etc.).

The chapter on financing a college education asks the reader to complete a worksheet estimating and comparing expenses at the different colleges being considered. It describes the financial options available (student employment, loans, scholarships, and grants) and lists where to write for more information.

Shortney, Joan Ranson: *How to Live on Nothing.* New York: Pocket Books, 1973.

Highly recommended by *The Whole Earth Catalogue* for its practical and accurate information this 320-page book suggests how to save money on the following topics: food, clothing, household furnishings, buying a house, maintenance and repair work, heating your house, gift-giving, vacationing, medicine, and knowing your social benefits. Information is thorough on each topic, and the reader is usually provided instructions for researching the topics discussed. Sometimes the reader is provided an inexpensive source of further information, such as a government publication.

The last chapter of the book consists of a list of 100 usually discarded objects and ways to reuse them. The good life, suggests the author, can be found by using the skills found in this book.

LEISURE

Lowery, Lucie: *Your Leisure Time . . . How to Enjoy It.* Los Angeles: Ward Richie Press, 1972.

Intended for those who live in the Los Angeles area, the book is also a useful guide for those living in other geographical areas. Following a brief discussion of the current status of leisure time, are seven chapters on various areas of leisure. Topics include high-risk leisure pursuits, artistic pursuits, scientific hobbies, physical activities, intellectual activities, volunteer activities, and off-beat leisure activities. Each chapter is punctuated with interesting stories about people who engage in the leisure activities discussed.

A "fun test" gives the reader his "leisure quotient." The book concludes with a list of people and organizations in the Los Angeles area which can assist in fulfilling one's leisure needs.

*Overs, Robert, Elizabeth O'Connor, Barbara DeMarco: *Guide to Avocational Activities.* Milwaukee, Wis.: Curative Workshop of Milwaukee, 1972.

This is a three-volume study which has provided a classification system for leisure activities. The system uses the following nine categories:

Games

Sports

Nature activities

Collection activities

Craft activities

Art and music activities

Education, entertainment, and cultural activities

Volunteer activities

Organizational activities

There are literally hundreds of activities briefly described in the three volumes. In addition to the description, each activity is rated according to environmental, social-psychological and cost factors. Of special interest to some readers is an indication of the extent to which various kinds of physical impairments limit doing each activity.

Schwartz, Alvin: *Hobbies: A Complete Guide to Crafts, Collections, Nature Study and Other Life-Long Pursuits.* New York: Simon & Schuster, 1972.
Author gives good overview of 27 leisure areas. Useful book to peruse at the library when you are considering starting a new leisure pursuit.

Yee, Min S., ed.: *The Great Escape.* New York: Bantam, 1974.
This very intriguing book is subtitled *A Source Book of Delights and Pleasures for the Mind and Body.* It is a compilation of facts, information, and ideas on how to escape from the ordinary. The book is loosely organized into the following escape areas. Just a sample of the escapes are noted:

Mind and body (martial arts, belly dancing, the occult)

Water (white-water rafting, sand trekking, swamp buggies)

Land (hikes, gold fever, skiing)

Nomadics (free travel, flying by thumb)

Places (ethnic places, U.S.A., country auctions)

Games (computer games, unusual games)

Each article gives enough description to hook the reader and enough information to get you to the next resource.

MARRIED, SINGLE, IN BETWEEN

Bach, George R. and Ronald M. Deutsch: *Pairing: How to Achieve Genuine Intimacy.* New York: Avon, 1970.
Dr. Bach has outlined the same type of techniques he described in another book, *The Intimate Enemy.* The techniques, developed and used at The Institute of Group Psychotherapy, rely heavily on the expression of

feelings in the here-and-now. Some of the techniques may appear rather "gimmicky." However, several of the suggestions and guidelines for effective communication procedures are useful. The authors have coined many words to describe "bad" nonintimate behavior (leveling, meditation) which at times detract from the instruction value of the book because one is caught up in lingo. The book does succeed in demonstrating that we often misread a person who is our intimate, and that the use of some fairly basic communication procedures can produce mutually satisfying results.

Baer, Jean: *The Second Wife.* New York: Pyramid, 1973.

In today's society many women will marry divorced men. This book outlines problems that women will likely face and discusses alternative solutions. Based on 220 interviews with second wives, the situations discussed include:

How to be a weekend stepmother.

How to be a full-time mother for his, mine, and ours.

How to deal with the legal and financial realities of the situation.

How to deal with the ex-wife in a variety of circumstances.

The book concludes by discussing why many second marriages fail. This is a useful book for those who are in or who contemplate entering a second marriage situation.

Bernard, Jessie: *The Future of Marriage.* New York: Bantam, Inc., 1972.

A very readable, but academic view of the past, present, and future of marriage. The author, a sociologist, has written a number of other books including *The Sex Game* and *The Academic Woman.*

When discussing the future of marriage, it is important to state whose marriage is being discussed—the husband's or the wife's. Considerable research shows that there are, in fact, two marriages in each union; and they often do not coincide.

After an interesting discussion of the history and current status of marriage, the author presents some other male and female writers' options for the future of marriage. These range from celibacy to communal neighborhoods. The author's own view is that marriage does have a future—a future of many options. These options will create many new demands, but the author does not state that the marriage partners will be happier or better adjusted than currently. She ends by making a plea to up-grade the wife's marriage.

Blaine, William L., and John Bishop: *Practical Guide for the Unmarried Couple.* New York: Two Continents Publishing Group, Ltd., 1976.

A very useful book if you are, or intend to, live as an unmarried couple. The book includes information for every category of unmarried couple—straight, gay, young or old. The authors, both attorneys, describe in a nontechnical, step-by-step approach how to deal with a wide range of matters including home buying, renting, wills, death, financial matters, and children. There is also a chapter on specific opportunities (e.g., tax breaks) available to the unmarried couple.

Casler, Lawrence: *Is Marriage Necessary?* New York: Popular, 1974.

The author contends this book is devoted to presenting the case against marriage—and he does it well. If you're considering marriage, divorce, or remarriage, this book should be of interest to you. Using research studies and opinions, the writer skillfully presents his case against the institution of monogamous marriage. His last chapter presents other alternatives. Thought-provoking.

Ellis, Albert: *The Sensuous Person.* New York: Signet, 1972.

If you've read other sex/technique books, you owe it to yourself to read *The Sensuous Person.* The author systematically questions the value of many of the popular sex manuals. He succeeds in making the reader a believer that the written word is not always true and, in fact, many times very misleading. This book helps give a balance to the current surge of interest in sexuality.

Johnson, Stephen M.: *First Person Singular: Living the Good Life Alone.* Philadelphia: Lippincott, 1977.

Even though the author contends this book is for all single people, the intended audience is newly-divorced singles. The three sections of the book cover: separating from the old relationship, how to live effectively alone, and establishing new relationships. The book has some good ideas.

Knox, David: *Marriage Happiness: A Behavioral Approach to Counseling.* Champaign, Ill.: Research Press, 1972.

This book is recommended to those who are considering marriage counseling which employs a behavioral approach. A behavioral approach is concerned with initiating and maintaining behavior which results in a happier marriage. For some people this approach makes a great deal of sense, and reading this book can prepare them for the relatively prescriptive techniques that will be utilized.

The first portion provides a general discussion of marital behavior. The underlying concept is that if the outcome (result) of the behavior is negative, the spouse is less likely to repeat it. If the outcome is positive, the spouse will more likely repeat it. Changing behavior then is the name of the game. The author outlines several techniques to change behavior, and describes how they can be used to resolve marital problems.

The author also devotes a chapter to each of the following marital problems: sex, communication, alcohol, in-laws, friends, religion, money, recreation, and children. The format in each of these chapters is similar. The author describes how behavioral techniques can be utilized to deal with the various problems.

The last section of the book is devoted to case studies from the author's experiences.

Krantzler, Mel: *Creative Divorce.* New York: Signet, 1974.

This book is pertinent to those both contemplating divorce and actually divorced. It emphasizes the commonality of feelings associated with divorce. You are not alone. Through the skillful use of case studies the author makes us aware of the concerns of the divorced. Guidelines for dealing with the issues are presented throughout the book.

Lederer, William J., and Don D. Jackson: *The Mirages of Marriage.* New York: Norton, 1968.

The Mirages of Marriage discusses marriage as it is, not as the romantics would realize it. After a brief description of the history of marriage, many of the false assumptions of modern marriage are identified. For example, the authors state that one false assumption is that loneliness will be cured by marriage.

Marriage is described as an interlocking system. The behavior of one spouse creates a reaction from the other spouse. At many times the behavior of one spouse conflicts with what the other desires (e.g., disagreement on which TV show to watch, where to go on a vacation, or how to spend a bonus). Specific techniques and exercises which help couples learn to negotiate are outlined.

The book also contains a marital checklist and a discussion on the use of marital counselors.

Lobsenz, Norman M., and Clark W. Blackburn: *How to Stay Married.* Greenwich, Conn.: Fawcett, 1969.

Two particularly valuable aspects of this book are: (1) the "no nonsense" approach to marriage that is illustrated, and (2) a presentation of the viewpoint and philosophy of the Family Service Association.

In regard to the first aspect, the book is believable. It tells it like it is. This is achieved in part, by the inclusion of examples of problems common to most marriages. In all of the topics dealt with such as in-laws, first adjustments, sex, money, communications, and role expectations, the authors give examples or case studies of the problem and offer general guidelines for solutions. No "cure all," but a readable, intelligent approach.

The second value of the book—acquainting one with the philosophy of

Family Service—is important to any couple contemplating using that service. A list of all the Family Service Associations by state is included.

Masters, William, and Virginia Johnson: *The Pleasure Bond.* Toronto: Bantam, 1976.

This is not a book about sexual techniques but rather a discussion about sex. A portion of the book consists of transcripts of tape-recorded discussion sessions facilitated by Masters and Johnson. The reader will probably find the openness and candor of the participants interesting and informative. One should read this book first *before* buying a "how-to" sex book.

Mazur, Ronald: *The New Intimacy.* Boston: Beacon Press, 1973.

Those readers who liked O'Neill's book *Open Marriage* will find that this book helps to describe more specifically the open-marriage concept. Through descriptions, probing questions, and end-of-the-chapter exercises you will probably discover more fully whether open marriage is for you.

O'Neill, Nena, and George O'Neill: *Open Marriage.* New York: Avon, 1973.

According to the authors, "open marriage means an honest and open relationship between two people, based on the equal freedom and identity of both partners. It involves a verbal, intellectual, and emotional commitment to the right of each to grow as an individual within the marriage." The authors identify eight cardinal guidelines to achieving an open marriage. These are:

Living for now and realistic expectations

Privacy

Open and honest communication

Flexibility in roles

Open companionship

Equality

Identity

Trust

The core of the book outlines methods for following the guidelines. The authors contend that achieving an open marriage is a "self-reinforcing, regenerative, and growth-enhancing system" that continues to expand.

Steinor, Bernard: *When Parents Divorce.* New York: Pocket Books, 1970.

The author's contention is that parents as well as children can grow emotionally through the process of divorce. He further believes that "the friendly divorce" recommended by many is not always the best option because it can lead to hypocrisy and phoniness. Instead, he proposes a psychological divorce or "divorce with freedom" that legitimately recognizes the differences between the parting couple.

This book is most useful to those contemplating divorce, not because it gives right answers but because it points up many of the issues which divorcing couples with children must face. Issues discussed include: reaching agreements on custody and property, telling the children about the divorce, problems of the custodial parent and the visitation parent, and considering dating and remarriage. The author advises that these issues be dealt with honestly and gives many specific examples of the problems that can arise within them.

OCCUPATIONAL PLANS AND OPPORTUNITIES

Career Planning

Beitz, Charles, and Michael Washburn: *Creating the Future.* New York: Bantam, 1974.

Subtitled *A Guide to Living and Working for Social Change,* the book is a very useful resource for those with such aspirations. The author claims that people can work for social change both within established institutions or through creating alternative institutions. An introductory section describes idealized communities in terms of services and governmental operations. Major concern is with specific areas of social change and how to find out more about these areas. Included are chapters on media, education, health, business, politics, science and technology, church, labor, and the federal government. Each chapter outlines social change possibilities and concludes with extensive resource lists of people, places, or things to contact for further information. If social change is your thing, this is a good buy!

Dictionary of Occupations Titles, vol. 1, *Definitions of Titles.* Washington: U.S. Government Printing Office, latest edition.

Volume 1 of the *Dictionary of Occupations Titles* has definitions of 35,500 job titles arranged alphabetically. The definitions are short (10-15 lines), and specific about job duties and responsibilities. The basic reference in occupational information.

*Forrester, Gertrude: *Occupational Literature: An Annotated Bibliography.* New York, H. W. Wilson, 1971.

A reference book to use in your local library for finding sources of information on specific occupations. Most of this 600-page volume is an annotated bibliography of books and pamphlets describing occupations. Occupations are listed alphabetically starting with *able seaman* and ending with *zoologist*. Under zoologist, for example, ten books and pamphlets are listed (prices included). Addresses of all publishers listed are included.

Various specialized bibliographies include: job seeking, occupations for the handicapped, planning a career, scholarships, professional counseling services, apprenticeships, and foreign study and employment.

The Graduate. Knoxville, Tennessee: Approach 13-30 Corporation, Annual.

An annual magazine for graduating college seniors subtitled *A Handbook for Leaving School.* Using the style and format of newstand publications, the brochure has more visual appeal than many other publications dealing with similar information. To order, send $2.00 to Approach 13-30 Corporation, 1005 Maryville Pike, S.W., Knoxville, Tennessee 37920.

Articles range in topics from job outlooks to issues faced by minority graduates to a special section on "The Real World Catalog." The latter section covers such items as arranging your finances, insurance, costs of moving, buying a stereo, and other "real world" facts. A helpful publication for the recent graduate.

McKee, Bill: *New Careers for Teachers.* Chicago: Regnery, 1972.

For a variety of reasons fewer positions are currently available for teachers. This book is intended to assist teachers find positions in teaching and nonteaching fields. The publication is divided into four sections:

1   A self-evaluation of interests, aptitudes, experience and knowledge

2   Descriptions of jobs for which little or no retraining would be necessary

3   The nitty-gritty of getting a job—résumés and interviews

4   Nontraditional careers in education

A good place to start for teachers who find they must (or want to) make a career change.

Occupational Outlook Handbook. Washington: U.S. Government Printing Office. Published biannually.

A reference available in most public libraries. More than 800 occupations are discussed in the *Handbook.* Each individual occupational listing, usually 2-3 pages, describes the nature of the work, places of employment, training, and other qualifications, advancement opportunities, employment outlook, earnings, and working conditions. Places to write for additional information are included at the end of each description. This reference is useful for all educational and age levels.

Splaver, Sarah: *Nontraditional College Routes to Careers*. New York: Messner, 1975.

A helpful listing of the new, nontraditional college education programs. It includes brief, but specific, information on correspondence study, study abroad, cooperative education, multimedia learning, nontraditional degree programs, and other innovations. The result to the reader should be that higher education is attainable and FUN.

*Teal Everett A. *The Occupational Thesaurus* (2 vols.). Bethelehem, Pa.: Lehigh University, 1971.

This reference set is designed to assist the reader to learn the job opportunities which exist for particular college majors. The following college majors are included: anthropology, economics, history, languages, mathematics, political science, psychology, sociology, accounting, biology, chemistry, finance, geology, management, marketing, physics, and transportation.

Entry occupations are listed for each of these major fields of study. The effect, particularly for the reader in liberal arts, is the realization that many options are available for those with undergraduate degrees.

Vocational Biographies. Sauk Centre, Minn.: Vocational Biographies, 1972.

The *Vocational Biographies* series is a helpful tool in career planning. Each series contains 6 volumes, and each volume has 25 four-page case histories describing the careers of people in the vocations spotlighted. Biographies conclude with specific job facts and places to write for further information.

The strength of *Vocational Biographies* is that information is presented in an interesting, involving manner. Blue-collar as well as white-collar occupations are included.

Vocational Guidance Manuals, 620 South Fifth Street, Louisville, Ky. 40202.

This publisher produces a series of books about specific vocational fields. Each book describes in detail current realities in the field. Titles include:

Opportunities in Forestry Careers

Opportunities in Environmental Careers

Opportunities in Publishing

Opportunities in Foreign Language Careers

Opportunities in Technical Writing Today

Opportunities in Graphic Communications

Opportunities in Carpentry Careers

A complete catalog of VGM books is available on request at no charge.

Weaver, Peter: *You, Inc.: A Detailed Escape Route to Being Your Own Boss.* Garden City, N.Y.: Dolphin, 1973.

The author started his own business after working 20 years for "the establishment." His book outlines the pitfalls but stresses the advantages of being on your own. The book combines "how-to-do-it" with interesting stories of those who have. A good place to start if you want your own ideas and creativity to guide your life.

International

*Angel, Juvenal L.: *Dictionary of American Firms Operating in Foreign Countries.* World Trade Academy Press, latest edition.

Includes data on more than 3,000 American corporations operating overseas. Arranged alphabetically with cross references both by geography and product. If you want to work overseas for a business, this source is the place to start.

*Calvert, Robert. *A Definitive Study of Your Future in International Service.* New York: Richard Rosen Press, 1969.

Contains a discussion of careers with religious, voluntary, and governmental organizations overseas. There is also a chapter on teaching opportunities abroad.

Hopkins, Robert. *I've Had It.* New York: Holt, 1972.

Subtitled "A Practical Guide to Moving Abroad," the book discusses the problems and advantages of moving abroad. The author relates the cycles that some people might experience if they actually make such a move. These include an initial period of elation, followed by a period of despondency and considering moving back to the U.S., and finally a period of leveling off when one realistically realizes the disadvantages and advantages in one's chosen environment. Information is included on job availability, taxes, climate, schools, and language training. Also included are lists of sources of books, pamphlets, and guides.

International Yellow Pages. New York: Donnelley.

Lists business and professional firms and individuals from 150 countries throughout the world under headings which are descriptive of the products and services they have to offer in world-wide trade. English, French, German, and Spanish language versions. Divided into six geographical areas: Africa, Asia, Australia and Oceania, Europe, Latin America and Caribbean, North America. Lists businesses and organizations of an international character.

Job Hunting

Bolles, Richard Nelson: *What Color is Your Parachute?* Berkeley, California: Ten Speed Press, 1973.

Subtitled, *A Practical Manual for Job-Hunters & Career Changers,* the book begins by describing why traditional strategies for job search are ineffective. The author discourages what he calls "the numbers game" approach to job hunting (e.g., sending out 100 resumes to get six job interviews).

Bolles' 3-step prescription for job search consists of:

1 Deciding just exactly what you want to do.
2 Deciding just exactly where you want to do it, through your own research and personal survey.
3 Researching the organizations that interest you at great length, and then approaching the one individual in each organization who has the power to hire you for the job that you have decided you want to do.

The remainder of the book describes exactly how to complete these three steps. This is one of the better "how-to" books on job searching.

Chamberlain, Betty: *The Artist's Guide to His Market.* New York: Watson-Guptill, 1975.

If you are an artist who has passed the rank of amateur, this is your book. It describes the ins and outs of working with a gallery, contractual agreements, pricing your work, publicity, and many other practical areas of concern to the self-employed artist.

Haldane, Bernard, Jean Haldane, and Lowell Martin: *Job Power Now: The Young People's Job Finding Guide.* Washington: Acropolis, 1976.

An excellent book for the younger job hunter. It assists the reader to analyze the skills he has accumulated in all aspects of his life and assists him in presenting this information to the potential employer.

Irish, Richard K: *Go Hire Yourself an Employer.* Garden City, N.Y.: Anchor, 1973.

A question and answer format is used in this "how-to-do-a-job-search" book. Traditional strategies of completing résumés and setting goals are covered. The author also makes the point that you, the employee, are really hiring an employer and thus it is up to you to interview the interviewer and negotiate your salary. Outlines for implementing this strategy are presented.

The last two chapters of the book deal with special employment situations (being a CO, a woman, a member of a minority group, handicapped) and opportunities with the federal government.

Jacquish, Michael P.: *Personal Résumé Preparation.* New York: Wiley, 1968.

An excellent guide for résumé preparation. The case for an effective résumé is made clearly. Four résumé formats are clearly discussed and illustrated (chronological, functional, organizational, and creative). The reader is helped to assess which is best for his/her particular situation. Several suggestions are given for dealing with sometimes "sticky" issues, such as, reason for leaving last position, age, desired salary, and marital status. Clear, concise information and illustrations are given on such considerations as the actual typing, paper, and printing specifications for the résumé. The last chapter details guidelines to use when writing cover letters. Examples of cover letters are included.

Larson, Darold E.: *How to Find a Job.* New York: Ace, 1974.

Well-organized book on the art of job hunting. A good beginning book when faced with a job-finding problem.

Nutter, Carolyn F.: *The Résumé Workbook.* Cranston, R.I.: Carroll Press, 1970.

As the title indicates, the approach of this "how-to book" is in workbook format. The introduction section describes and illustrates four kinds of résumés which are the chronological, analytical, functional, and imaginative approaches. The next section of the workbook illustrates what résumé might be most appropriate for a specific job-hunting situation, such as mature woman, graduating college senior, military retiree, and high school graduate.

Research Aids

*Colgate, Craig, ed.: *1976 National Trade and Professional Associations of the United States and Canada and Labor Unions.* Washington: Columbia Books, annual.

This directory lists 5,700 organizations. A very good job-searching and career-planning aid because it indexes the organizations alphabetically, geographically, by name of executives in the corporation, by amount of budget the organization has, and by the type of product or field with which the organization is concerned.

College Placement Annual. Bethlehem, Pa.: College Placement Council, Inc. Published annually.

This reference is available at college placement offices as well as many public libraries. One of the most useful tools for any college graduate seeking employment, the *Annual* contains information on United States employers that hire college graduates. Information given on each employer includes the following: brief description of the nature of the business or organization, name of the college recruiting officer, number of employees, and occupational openings for which the organization will recruit. The *Annual* is indexed by academic disciplines and geographical areas.

Directory of Public Service Internships: Opportunities for the Graduate, Post-Graduate, and Mid-Career Professional. Washington: National Center for Public Service Internship Programs.

This directory, which intends to revise yearly, is a listing of public service agency programs designed for the postcollege grad. A one- or two-page program description outlines and describes admission requirements.

Encyclopedia of Associations. vol. I: *National Organizations of the U.S.* Detroit: Gale Research Co., latest edition.

A comprehensive list of all types of national associations arranged by broad classification, and with an alphabetical and keyword index. Gives names of chief officer, brief statements of activities, number of members, names of publications, etc. National associations can often give useful career planning information as well as specific help in a job search.

Encyclopedia of Business Information Sources. (2 vols.) Detroit: Gale Research Co., latest edition.

This two-volume encyclopedia is a good beginning source to use to find out where to seek further information on a business topic. The first volume is arranged alphabetically and the topics range from abrasives industry to zoological gardens. Under each topic specific statistical sources, price sources, handbooks and manuals, periodicals, and trade associations are listed for further information. The contents in volume 2 are for those interested in international business information, and the contents are arranged by geographical location from Africa to Zanzibar.

Federal Career Directory: A Guide for College Students. Washington: United States Civil Service Commission, latest edition.

If you want to consider the federal government as an employer and you have an undergraduate college degree, start with this publication. It should be available in your local library or in any college placement office. The *Directory* is divided into three parts:

1   Description of federal career occupations

2   Description of federal agencies

3   Job briefs listed by college major

Read this before taking the Federal Service Entrance Examination.

For those who have a graduate degree contact your regional Federal Job Information Center and ask for information about mid-level positions in your area of specialty. Those with a community college degree or high school diploma should contact the Information Center for publications relevant to your background and experience.

Greenfield, Phyllis O.: *Educator's Placement Guide.* National Center for Information on Careers in Education, 1972.

This small guide gives a wealth of information, including:

Current trends in educational staffing needs

Addresses for certification information by state

Services of state education associations

Services of professional and private agencies

Addresses of independent, federal, international, and innovative schools

Information on nonteaching careers (e.g., educational publishing houses, regional educational labs, research centers)

Sample application letters and résumés

Industrial Research Laboratories of the United States. Washington, D.C., National Research Council. Published annually.

Contains information on 5,237 nongovernmental laboratories devoted to fundamental and applied research, and operated by 3,115 organizations, mostly industrial firms. It includes fields of research interest and names of research and development executives. There are both subject and geographical indexes. Those with a science or technical background will particularly find this helpful for names of potential employers.

Lewis, M., ed.: The Foundation Directory. New York: Columbia, 1971.

Directory of nongovernmental, nonprofit organizations established to maintain or aid social, educational, charitable, religious or other activities serving the common welfare. The two criteria for inclusion in the directory are: (1) awarded grants of $25,000 or more in that year, (2) total assets of $500,000 or more. This directory is useful in investigating foundations as potential employers, and also for preparation of proposals for grants to determine possible support. It is indexed alphabetically by state and by fields of interests.

MacMillan Job Guide to American Corporations. New York: MacMillan, 1967.

The guide offers a broad look at major American corporations—their goals, personnel requirements, and opportunities. Four areas covered in the guide include:

Description of corporations and job opportunities. (This includes information on annual sales, employees, mission and products, facilities, degree requirements and opportunities and benefits.)

Alphabetical index to corporations

Index to corporations by college degrees

Geographical index to home offices

This book is a good place to start to find out what companies are seeking persons with a particular type of college background.

*Pingree, E., ed.: *Business Periodicals Index*. New York: H. W. Wilson, latest edition.

Indexes approximately 250-300 journals covering a wide range of industries. Excellent general reference for researching a company or an industry. It is indexed alphabetically by company and by industry, and it lists all articles within a given year relating to a particular company or industry. The index is also useful for identifying trade journals for a given field.

Research Centers Directory, 3d ed., Detroit: Gale Research Co., 1968.

A directory of apporximately 4,500 research institutes, centers, foundations, laboratories, bureaus, and other nonprofit research facilities in the U.S. and Canada. It is arranged by type of research done. Excellent for identifying research organizations in any field (social science, education, biological science, physical science, business and industrial relations, etc.). Information includes scope of research activities and names of publications, sources of funding and names and addresses of principal researchers. This directory would be helpful to those wanting to work in a particular research area or for identifying names of people who could be helpful in a job search.

Thomas Register of American Manufacturers. New York: Thomas Publishing, 1971.

These eleven volumes contain detailed information on leading manufacturers throughout the country. Included in the volumes are:

Vol. 1-6 Products and services listed alphabetically

Vol. 7 Company names, addresses and telephone numbers with Capital ratings, names of company officials, and locations of branch offices

Vol. 8 Brand names

Vol. 9-11 Catalogs of companies appearing alphabetically and cross-indexed in first 8 volumes

*Wasserman, Paul and W. R. Greer, Jr.: *Consultants and Consulting Organizations.* New York: Graduate School of Business and Public Administration, Cornell University, 1966.

This is a detailed listing of consulting firms arranged alphabetically and cross-referenced by subject field and geographical location. This could be helpful in a job search in locating companies doing independent consulting in your area of expertise. They could be considered potential employers, or persons who could describe the feasibility of starting your own consulting firm.

West Coast Theatrical Dictionary. Los Angeles: Tarcher/Gousha Guides, 1971.

Contains information on companies related to the entertainment industry in Los Angeles, San Francisco, Nevada, and Hawaii. There are also alphabetical listings for Chicago, Nashville, and New York. The main sections of the directory include: artists' representatives; broadcastin/radio and television and associated services; live show production and distribution; motion picture and TV production equipment, facilities, and services; music, recording, tape, and associated services; theatrical instruction; and unions, guilds, and trade associations. For those interested in the entertainment industry this is a good source.

Women

Fairbank, Jane D., and Helen L. Bryson: *Second Careers for Women.* Second Careers for Women: Calif.: Stanford, 1975.

This book is written for women in the San Francisco Bay area, but much of the information is applicable to a wider audience. The Second Careers series gives descriptive information about a wide range of career fields and their applicability as a second career for women.

Friedman, Sande, and Lois Schwartz: *No Experience Necessary: A Guide to Employment for the Female Liberal Arts Graduate.* New York: Dell, 1971.

An excellent guide for the female college graduate who is uncertain about what she can or wants to do in the work world. The biggest portion of the book consists of fourteen chapters describing career fields that are most accessible to females with liberal arts degrees. Fields include: advertising, the art world, banking and finance, book publishing, government, magazine and newspaper publishing, nonprofit, personnel and training, public relations, television, radio, and travel. Each chapter includes a general description of the field and notes several illustrative positions. Information is also given on which beginning positions are most likely available, advancement possibilities, and salary ranges. Each chapter lists specific sources of further information. Job hunting techniques and part-time employment possibilities are both given some attention.

Higginson, Margaret, and Thomas L. Quick: *The Ambitious Woman's Guide to a Successful Career.* New York: Amacom, 1975.

A book for the woman who believes her place is not in the home but up the career ladder. Specific hints and information on how to be a success in the corporate world.

Place, Irene, and Alice Armstrong: *Management Careers for Women.* Louisville, Ky.: Vocational Guidance Manuals, Inc., 1975.

The authors have tried to combine a little of everything a woman needs to know to consider being a manager in today's economy and society. This ranges from brief descriptions of management theories, to common stereotypes of women in management, to a self-analysis rating. For those women just considering a management career, this might be a starter book.

Planning for Work. New York: Catalyst, 1973.

One of a series of booklets written by Catalyst, "the national nonprofit organization dedicated to expanding employment opportunities for college-educated women who wish to combine career and family responsibilities." Written in a self-guidance workbook format.

Scofield, Nanette E., and Betty Klarman: *So You Want to Go Back to Work!* New York: Random House, 1968.

A good general guide for the mature woman considering work options. The book starts by discussing the question common to women contemplating going back to work, viz., can I manage the house and care for the family's needs? The next section of the book asks readers to analyze their own situation and assess their strengths and weaknesses and outlines a number of ways to make a tentative career plan. Next, the most common career fields are described and ways to get further information are suggested.

The main portion of the book deals with the options open to the mature woman. Chapters are included on: returning to school, getting a full-time job, starting a business at home, getting a part-time job, and volunteering. Each of these options is carefully considered and examined from the perspective of the problems that would be encountered by the middle-aged wife/mother. For example, in discussing the option of returning to school, consideration is given to various types of school programs including continuing education, adult education, extension programs and home study. The implications of the effects of each alternative regarding home responsibilities are examined.

A planning approach is emphasized throughout the book. Women are encouraged to determine their goals, obtain the necessary information, anticipate the results of their actions, and make alternative plans to meet both their needs and the needs of the family.

Splaver, Sarah: *Nontraditional Careers for Women.* New York, Messner, 1963.

A brief, but effective, overview of 500 occupations which women may consider. The book's readability is enhanced by brief success stories of women in nontraditional fields.

The New Woman's Survival Sourcebook. New York: Knopf, 1975.

This 245-page guidebook describes and lists resources for many concerns of today's women, including work, money, health, children, sports, education, legal issues, literature, the arts, and religion and spirituality.

PARENTING

Biller, Henry, and Dennis Meredith: *Father Power.* New York: Anchor, 1975.

This book is meant to fill a void created by existing parenting books which primarily focus on the mother. The father's role in such developmental tasks as self-confidence, morals, social relationships, physical growth, sex identity, and intelligence is outlined and described via many examples. The special challenges of divorced fathers, stepfathers, handicapped fathers, and fathers of problem children are dealt with in the last section of the book.

Corsini, Raymond, and Genevieve Painter: *The Practical Parent: ABC's of Child Discipline.* New York: Harper & Row, 1975.

An excellent book for parents. After an introduction to the Adlerian approach to child guidance, the book deals specifically with many problems parents face. Sample problems include getting up, dressing, eating, keeping clean, bedtime, fighting in the car, temper tantrums, and many others. Each problem is discussed, solutions suggested, and case studies illustrated. An easy-to-read, sensible, practical book!

Dreikurs, Rudolf, with Vicki Soltz: *Children: The Challenge.* New York: Hawthorne, 1964.

An easy to read self-help presentation of Adlerian-Dreikursian approach to resolving parent-child conflicts. The book is directed primarily towards developing skills in handling oneself when in conflict with children eleven years of age and younger. However, the principles apply to any age level of relationship. Examples clarify the various principles presented. The appendix includes a series of exercises for testing the extent to which the reader has mastered the skills described in the text.

Soltz, Vicki: *Study Groups Manual.* Chicago: Alfred Adler Institute, 1967.

A manual designed to assist parent study group leaders in coordinating the information appearing in *Children: The Challenge* with study group deliberations. Especially suited to assisting lay leaders who have a propensity for "leadership" but need assistance in organizing the particular content. Includes techniques for leadership, study topic outlines, and discussion-promotion questions.

Dotson, Fitzhugh: *How to Parent.* New York: New American Library, 1970.

A collection of suggestions and advice regarding how to be an effective parent of children from birth through age five. Dotson believes that while parenting is one of the most complex and important occupations in our society, our educational system provides no formal training. His book is an attempt to provide some of that training. Especially helpful are appendices listing toys and play equipment, free and inexpensive toys, and a parents' guide to children's books for preschool children.

Ginott, Haim: *Between Parent and Child.* New York: Avon, 1969.

Written in a light, easy-to-read style, *Between Parent and Child* proposes that communication is the key to "settling the undeclared wars which so often leave both parents and child angry, confused, and regretful." The volume contains many specific examples of using open communication to solve specific problems. It could be particularly helpful for parents who truly don't understand why their children behave as they do. The examples are realistic and most parents will be able to experiment with some of Ginott's suggestions.

————*Between Parent and Teenager.* New York: Macmillan, 1969.

Very similar to Ginott's *Between Parent and Child* except the focus is on problems likely to arise during adolescence including rebellion, authority, conflict and crisis, identity and autonomy.

Gordon, Thomas: *Parent Effectiveness Training.* New York: Peter H. Widen, 1970.

Like many other books about parent-child conflict, this one strongly emphasizes communication. It describes and illustrates several methods for resolving parent-child problems and conflicts. Basic to parent effectiveness training is the concept of democratic discipline, wherein family rules are established which are acceptable to parents and children alike. Gordon's examination of concepts such as authority and discipline should be revealing, thought-provoking, and helpful to many parents.

Whelan, Elizabeth: *A Baby? . . . Maybe: A Guide to Making the Most Fateful Decision of Your Life.* New York: Bobbs-Merrill, 1975.

An excellent book for the person trying to decide whether to have a baby—or a second or third child. The book takes neither a pro- nor con-parenthood stance. Instead it gives facts and opinions on both sides and gives many questions for the reader to ponder. The author makes liberal use of case studies which makes a very personal approach to the topic.

RETIREMENT

Adler, Joan: *The Retirement Book.* New York: Morrow, 1975.

This book covers four primary areas of interest regarding retirement: financing, where to live, how to spend your time, and how to keep fit. Although this book is written in a less than interesting style, it gives specific, helpful information, and it has perhaps the best resource lists for further information and reading on all topics covered.

Arthur, Julietta K: *Retire to Action: A Guide to Voluntary Service.* Nashville, Abingdon, 1969.

Today's retirees are of the work-oriented generation so that suggestions in this volume may mean more than all the guides on recreational opportunities. The author has done a very thorough job of exploring volunteer opportunities and the information resources available to the retiree.

For those who are accustomed to viewing volunteering as envelope-stuffing, there may be some exciting vistas—even VISTA.

Collings, Kent J.: *The Second Time Around: Finding a Civilian Career in Mid-Life.* Cranston, R.I.: Carroll Press, 1971.

As the title indicates, this book is on target for a special population—the retired military. Much of what Mr. Collings has learned since his own retirement, however, is useful to the increasing numbers of the middle-aged who are looking for changes. Because Mr. Collings' style is spritely, his observations acute, and his honesty refreshing, this book is fun to read, retiree or not.

Comfort, Alex: *A Good Age.* New York: Crown, 1976.

Mr. Comfort, who wrote *The Joy of Sex,* uses the same laundry-list style of writing for this book. It is an excellent book to get your "head straight" about aging. This is not a "how-to" book like the rest on the list, but it gives good information and assists in changing the reader's attitude about aging.

Cooley, Leland Frederick, and Lee M. Cooley: *The Retirement Trap.* Garden City, N.J.: Doubleday, 1965.

The Cooleys are out to instruct the unwary on the pitfalls in retirement, primarily housing choices. However, as in most retirement guides, the concern is life style. "Through darkest retirement with gimlet and screwdriver," says the bartender in one retirement village when he characterizes the lost souls he "counsels." The need to be needed cannot be dismissed lightly. Retirement villages, they believe, are filled with the unneeded.

Dickinson, Peter: *The Complete Retirement Planning Book.* New York: Dutton, 1976.

An excellent book! The author has written about a wide range of topics in an easily readable, fact-filled manner. The end result for the reader is a sense that one can plan what will happen in retirement years, and that it can be an enjoyable, challenging process.

Hart, Mollie: *When Your Husband Retires.* New York: Appleton-Century-Crofts, 1960.

While most retirement preparation books are written for the employed person, this one, as the title indicates, aims at helping wives anticipate retirement irritations. The author writes, "From now on this is going to happen every day. Not just Saturday and Sunday but every Saturday and Sunday and every other day of the week too—forever. Wow!"

Hepner, Harry W.: *Retirement—A Time to Live Anew.* New York: McGraw-Hill, 1969.

This is one of the best books available on retirement planning. It is addressed primarily to the businessmen who have no great worries about retirement income. Written by a retired psychology professor, the book is a gold mine of information, guidance, and good sense. Mr. Hepner's ability to provoke sound thinking should be of great value to all persons approaching retirement so that they can plan on a realistic and effective basis for the later years. It can be equally helpful and stimulating to those already retired.

McKain, Walter C.: *Retirement Marriage.* Storrs, Conn.: Storrs Agricultural Experiment Station. University of Connecticut, 1969.

Marriage at sixty plus is not a subject about which much is written. This report of research is presented in lay language. Indicators for success of late-life marriage are listed and the book includes a self-administered test for predicting successful retirement marriage.

Morrison, Morie: *Retirement in the West.* San Francisco: Chronicle Books, 1976.

For those wanting to go Westward Ho, this book gives general and specific information on communities in eleven states. Included is information on climate, housing availability, medical services, living costs, extra-income sources, and senior-citizen organizations.

Olmstead, Alan H.: *Threshold: The First Days of Retirement.* New York: Harper & Row, 1975.

This book chronicles the first six months of the author's retirement. An interesting record that describes the highs and lows—the important and trivial. It increases the reader's awareness of this time in one's life. This is not a "how-to book," but well worth reading and reflecting on.

Staley, Mark J., and Ralph H. Singleton: *Dynamic Retirement.* Cleveland: Uniline Co., 1966.

This book, more than other retirement books, assists readers to psychologically "get their games together." The practical realities of health and finance are also dealt with very well, but essentially it's the book's purpose to assist you to explore your own needs and values. The book assists with this planning with fifteen very well designed worksheets.

EXERCISES

1 Information is power—not original but true. Read the annotated bibliography and check those of interest to you or to others you might help. Check your public library to see if your checked books are there.

2 The bibliography has seven sections: Education, Finances, Leisure, Marriage, Occupational Plans, Parenting, and Retirement. Choose one of these areas that is of most interest to you and go to your local library and add to the existing entries in the bibliography. Keep it updated for future use.

3 Another project, which may be more costly, is starting your own library collection in one of the areas.

Index

218 INDEX